EVERYDAY PRAYERS

EVERYDAY PRAYERS

Contributors
ALLEN BIRTWHISTLE
BERNARD THOROGOOD
MICHAEL WALKER

Editor
HAZEL SNASHALL

INTERNATIONAL BIBLE READING ASSOCIATION
National Christian Education Council
Robert Denholm House
Nutfield, Redhill, Surrey, RH1 4HW

ACKNOWLEDGEMENTS

We are grateful for permission to include the following:

Verse 1 of the hymn *Have faith in God, my heart* by Bryn Rees, on page 8;

Verse 5 of the hymn *Once from a European shore* by Brian Wren (Oxford University Press) on page 20;

Extract from *The Secular City* by Harvey Cox (SCM Press) on page 34;

Extract from the *Methodist Covenant Service* (Methodist Publishing House) on page 48;

Verses from the *New English Bible* ©1970 (Oxford and Cambridge University Presses);

Verses from the *Good News Bible* (GNB) ©American Bible Society, New York, 1976 (The Bible Societies/Collins Publishers);

Verses from the *Living Bible* (LB) (Coverdale House Publishers Ltd);

Verses from the *New Testament in Modern English* (JBP) by J.B. Phillips (Collins Publishers);

Verses from the *Revised Standard Version* (RSV) ©1946 and 1952 Division of Christian Education, National Council of Churches of Christ in the USA.

Biblical quotations are from the New English Bible unless otherwise indicated.

Cover photo: Nicholas Servian FIIP, Woodmansterne Limited

0 7197 0213 5

Typeset by Surrey Graphics Ltd, Dorking, Surrey
Printed and bound by Cox & Wyman Ltd, Fakenham, Norfolk

CONTENTS

INTRODUCTION

Personal prayer and devotion is an essential part of Christian life and experience. Yet for many Christians it is not easy to undertake and sustain the discipline of prayer. This book is designed to be of help by suggesting a variety of themes for prayer which can be used over a period of time.

The first two sections provide daily devotional material, while the third section contains material for the special seasons of the Christian year. Because our personal circumstances are so varied it is not possible to provide prayers for every occasion but there are many experiences of life which are common to most of us. The final section of this book is designed to be of help when such common needs arise, and the prayers can be used during daily devotions or just when required.

The pattern of the book is to start each day with praise, followed by a meditation or prayers related to the theme of the day. If the Bible is being read during these devotions, it is suggested that the appropriate point would be immediately following the opening praise.

No book of prayers can ever adequately express the full depth of personal faith and devotion but the contributors to this book have drawn on their wide-ranging and distinctive experiences, and offer these prayers and devotions to be a help and guide to those who will use them.

The Revd Bernard Thorogood is a minister of the United Reformed Church, the Revd Allen Birtwhistle is a Methodist minister, and the Revd Michael Walker a Baptist minister.

FAITH, HOPE AND LOVE

Thanksgiving for the seed of faith   Day 1

Have faith in God, my heart,
Trust and be unafraid;
God will fulfil in every part
Each promise he has made.   *Bryn Rees*

Through faith you are all sons of God in union with Christ Jesus.
(Galatians 3.26)

Father, I thank you for giving me faith,
for that is the foundation of my prayers.
I believe that I am your child,
living in your world in your day.
My faith is shaky and suffers many knocks.
There are times when I push you out of my mind
and days when I cannot hear your voice.
Yet deep in my heart I believe in you,
your abiding, your holy love.
Thank you for giving me that seed of faith.

As I pray, I know that the little seed
is also fruit of a great tree of faith,
which stretches across the years and the continents
and links me to the apostles.

Great God, faith is the powerful bond
which links all Christian people.
We praise you for faith and faithfulness
    in the ages of darkness,
    in disappointments and disasters,
    in hostile societies where faith is called madness,
    amid affluent agnostics,
    expressed in every human language,
    victorious in pain and in death,
this is the work of your Spirit.
May this great tree of faith continue to grow,
deeply rooted in your word,
and offering to all a living faith
for the healing of the nations.

We all interpret Jesus through our own experience.

John the Baptist said, 'Behold, the Lamb of God!' To Nathanael he was 'Rabbi', to Peter 'Messiah', to John 'Logos'.

So today the Christian revolutionary sees Jesus as his leader, while teachers see in Jesus the supreme teacher. Is this strange?

Lord God, you give us Jesus,
you come to the world in the form we understand,
you travel with us the journey from birth to death.
Help us to know and trust in Jesus our brother
that we may enter into his way of obedience
and, having passed through the tests of life,
join in your feast of joy at the end.   Amen

Father, I look at Jesus and see what I long to be.
I am tired and I see in him your creative energy;
I care what people think of me, but Jesus went on his way, ready
to be laughed at;
I miss so often the real longing in the words of my friends, but
Jesus knows the heart;
I fear the future, but I see Jesus setting his face to go up to
Jerusalem.
Thank you, Father, for Jesus our brother,
revealing human nature as you created it to be,
and staying with us in all our days.

Pray for all those who can see no god but only blind fate, only the blundering machine.

O God, have mercy on your bewildered children,
that in the midst of this alarming world
they may recognise in Jesus your personal care
and your presence to heal and save.
May we be agents of that care and that presence,
in spite of the little we can do, because we know Jesus.

> *My dear Almighty Lord,*
> *My Conqueror and my King,*
> *Thy sceptre and thy sword,*
> *Thy reigning grace I sing.*
> *Thine is the power: behold I sit*
> *In willing bonds before thy feet.*   *Isaac Watts*

Dear Lord of my home and my affections,
   of my timetable and my appetites,
   of my possessions and my dreams,
      I would follow you.

Great Lord of Catholic, Protestant and Orthodox,
   of black and white and coloured,
   of generations past and future,
      I would obey you.

Wise Lord of the kings and rulers,
   of Caesar and Pilate and Herod,
   of Chairman Mao and Mahatma Gandhi,
   of philosophers and generals,
      I would honour you.

Loving Lord of the teenager playing with drugs,
   of the meths drinker down and out,
   of the Indian coolie near starvation,
   of weary miner and distant fisherman,
      I would work for you.

Lord, King of glory, inspirer, healer, Saviour,
Jesus the Christ, crowned with thorns,
speaking the word with authority to my heart,
be Lord this day and Lord for ever.   Amen

Pray for any you know who are in positions of authority, that they may be willing to be led by the Spirit of God and learn the limits of human power.

*I tell you that whoever does not accept the kingdom of God like a
child will never enter it.
When you pray, say, 'Father....'*   (*Luke 18.17; 11.2*)

A prayer of confession
Father, so often I do not think of you like that,
nor do I know myself to be your child.
Instead you seem more distant than the sun,
ancient, vague, impossible to know.
I fail to hear the father's voice
and in your presence I am not at home.
Father, how can I speak to you?
Father, how can I trust your love?
Help me now, in the power of the Spirit,
to say this word, and mean it: Father.

Rejoicing in the fatherhood of God
How wonderful it is, Father, that all of life
finds its source in you.
Behind the world of nature, spider's web
and wind-blown wave, lava flow
and night sky filled with stars;
Behind the world of human life,
athletic skill and author's pen,
politician's promise and mother's patient care,
child's sudden smile and miner's black-faced grin;
Behind the world of the imagination,
visions of beauty made permanent on canvas
and melody that sings in the mind;
Behind it all, the lovely and the cruel,
the simple and the complex, is one creating spirit,
you, our Father, Creator, Sustainer and Healer of life.
May your children rejoice in your power
and proclaim your love to the ends of the earth.

*Praise the Lord, my soul.
As long as I live I will praise the Lord;
I will sing psalms to my God all my life long.
O praise the Lord.*   (*Psalm 146.1-2*)

11

Elijah mocked them: 'Call louder, for he is a god; it may be he is deep in thought, or engaged, or on a journey; or he may have gone to sleep and must be woken up.' (*1 Kings 18.27*)

Elijah was laughing at the futility of praying to the Baals, idols without life.
The Christian rejoices in the God who speaks.

Praise be to God for the word of wisdom
 which challenges our shallow thoughts
 and our unconscious habits.
Praise be to God for the word of prophecy
 which punctures our respectability
 and shows us the world we shall make
 if we stay as we are.
Praise be to God for the word of history,
 for real people finding their way
 and seeking the kingdom.
Praise be to God for the living Word, Jesus,
 who speaks by the way he lived
 and the way he cared, by the road
 to Jerusalem and on to Golgotha.
Praise be to God for the word in the Church,
 through bread and wine,
 through the water of baptism,
 through the voice of the saints,
 through faithful preachers of the word.
For every word of God we give thanks
and pray that we may have ears and hearts open to hear,
through Christ our Lord.

Pray for those who translate, print and spread the Bible throughout the world, and ask that this work may be done with skill and with faith.

Speak, Lord, your servant hears you.

Quietly, but with assurance, Jesus said 'For this I was born; for this I came into the world, and all who are not deaf to truth listen to my voice.' Then Pilate, in a tone of weariness and disillusion, commented, 'What is truth?', and went out again to the crowd to bargain over the life of Jesus.

So through the ages those who long for truth, who hunger for truth like starving people, who cling to truth with mind and heart meet the careless ones whose lives are ruled by expediency.

As Christians we have no choice but to fight for truth; this is the freedom of the spirit, to launch out without a lifebelt in a rough sea. Yet for all of us the search goes on as long as life lasts.

Heavenly Father, you have put into our hearts the longing to find out the truth, now enable us, in all the joys and sorrows of life, to discover what is the depth of your purpose and the power of your presence, even to the pain of the cross; through Christ our risen Lord.   Amen

A prayer for those who wander in their search
Dear God, the eternal home of ourselves, our minds and our hearts, we bring to you all your children who seek truth far from Bethlehem and Calvary;
    those who look to eastern mysticism,
    those who put their trust in Marxism,
    those who, almost lost, seek a glimpse of truth through drugs,
    those who see truth only in acts of violence,
    and those, closer to us, who think that truth is another word for
       success.

We pray that, by grace, your gospel may be a light to these wandering children of your love. May they see themselves in the light of your truth, and turn to you.

> *Has his steadfast love for ever ceased?*
>   *Are his promises at an end for all time?*
> *Has God forgotten to be gracious?*
> *I will call to mind the deeds of the Lord.*
> *Thy way, O God, is holy.*
>   *What god is great like our God?*
>
>   *(Psalm 77.8-9,11,13, RSV)*

So faith and doubt seem to belong together in our experience.
On the day of resurrection 'some doubted', and through the ages
the saints have wrestled with doubt.

Father, I have doubts about myself.
I wonder how honest I really am,
for I can often use the lovely words of faith
when experience is not like the words.
I have doubts about my progress in the faith,
for when I look back I see a courage and
enthusiasm which today I lack.
I have doubts about my prayers,
wondering if I just talk to myself.
     Lord, in my doubts, remind me of your deeds,
        your way of healing, your word of power.
And, Father, I am part of an age of doubters.
I find it very easy to doubt the integrity of
people in public life.
I cannot give unquestioning obedience
even to my church authorities whom I respect,
and I doubt the words of the ancient creeds.
     Lord, in my doubts may I know you are to be trusted, when
        all else is shaken.

Pray for those who are bewildered and cynical
Lord God, foundation of life and sustainer of the world, may your
lost children find assurance that you live, that you love; and may
this be the rock on which life is given new joy, through Jesus
Christ our Lord.

We praise you, Lord God, because you are known to us in Jesus Christ. We wonder at your gift of the Spirit. But though we know you, you are beyond us.
We praise you, beyond our reach, outside our control.
We praise you, for when we have wrestled with you, you have prevailed.

So we think today of people of other faiths, and we confess that we approach them in such ignorance.

There are faiths which also look towards the Holy Land,
Judaism and Islam, uneasy neighbours,
but strong systems of belief and discipline,
lasting through the years and through persecution,
proclaiming one God.
    Lord, what truth there is in them, you know.
    Help us first to learn and to love,
    and so to share the truth that is in Christ.

There are faiths which seem very far from us,
Hinduism with its multitude of gods,
its strange idols, homely shrines and fixed social system;
the path of the Buddha, so quiet, so peaceful,
washing away the troubles and the passions
of the patient disciple.
    Lord, what truth there is in these, you know.
    Help us first to learn and to love,
    and so to share the truth that is in Christ.

Father, there are many other ways in which men and women seek to touch eternity.
We ask for your help that we may learn to live together in this world which is our home, and, in the world which is your kingdom, to know the mystery of your great glory, through Jesus Christ.

To many of us there seem to be two quite separate compartments in life today. Our religious feelings and ideas and aims are in one part of life, and our technical abilities and tasks in quite another. Perhaps we fear that God is in the old-fashioned compartment, due to fade away.

God, you know all the wonders of this age
and the skills in our human minds and hands;
you have cared for us through all of history;
therefore I pray:
    help us to use technology for the good of people,
    to heal those who have come close to despair,
    to ease the life of those in pain,
    to build good homes for those who live in shacks,
    to bring fertility to the deserts
    and good crops to our farms,
    to let the blind see again.
So may our technical marvels be your hand at work in our world.
Forgive all those who use the power of modern communications to spread a false picture of the world, and forgive us all that we have lacked discrimination to select what is good and reject what betrays you, through Jesus Christ.   Amen

A prayer for those who are fearful
Dear Father, we used to be afraid of evolution,
afraid that it would destroy the Bible and the faith.
But what truth there is in the unfolding history
of life on earth is your truth.
So today, when we hear about nuclear energy,
and transplant surgery, and men in space,
may we remember that space, life and energy
are all part of your good creation.
Always and everywhere you are God.

Thy hands gave me shape and made me;
and dost thou at once turn and destroy me?
Remember that thou didst knead me like clay;
and wouldst thou then turn me back into dust?

(Job 10.8-9)

'One cup of rice is all we can allow.'
The eyes look back in hunger and in pain,
Wide, deep brown eyes sunken beneath the brow
Pulled taut by famine in a world insane.
The rip of water tearing through the plain
Leaves goats and people islanded on hills;
They come to fear the never ending rain
And curse the Lord who will not pay their bills.
Too rapidly the face of earth now fills
With myriad faces, each demanding, 'Why
Do I not count?' Enormous crisis kills
Our understanding; need defeats supply.
The Buddha smiles; in him no tears I trace.
Stay with us Christ, we need your crisis face.

Lord God, at the moment of my falling
    hold me and save me, in Jesus Christ.
Lord God, when there is ultimate loneliness
    be present to befriend me, in Jesus Christ.
Lord God, when my world is in chaos
    enable me to see your plan, in Jesus Christ.
Lord God, when I see my neighbours are starving
    help me to share all I have, in Jesus Christ.
Lord God, at the moment of violence, anger, blood,
    take hate from my heart, in Jesus Christ.
Lord God, when the shadow of death is near me
    give me the life which is in Jesus Christ.

By thy saving power, O God, lift me high
above my pain and my distress.   *(Psalm 69.29)*

17

We listen to some prayers of children:
'O God, let me become a grown-up soon, so that
I can do anything I want to do.'
'Father God, do you hear my little brother crying?
If you do, can't you stop him and make him laugh?'
'God, some people say that you don't live in outer space.
Help me to go there, so I can find out.'
'God, are you like my father? Is that why they
call you Father, too?'

How often we are stirred, challenged, delighted and given new
hope by the children we know.

Father, thank you for new life, new beginning
in every child, for there we see your constant love.
Thank you for the energy and gaiety of children,
reminding us that we live in a fascinating world.
Thank you for the questions children ask,
for enquiring minds and for growth,
because there we see hope for tomorrow.
Thank you for the laughter and tears of children,
reminding us that dark and light
are both parts of your good creation.

Lord God, I need to confess to you that sometimes I am so
irritated by the noise and the demands of children that I lose
patience and drive them away.
I confess also the cruelty still seen in our country, and which I
know lurks in a corner of my heart.
Forgive, heal, give understanding; through Christ.

Intercession for handicapped children
Loving Father, we remember in your presence all children who
are crippled or deformed in body or mind or spirit. Guard those
who care for them. Strengthen those who seek to heal them. Lead
us all to make real your love for them.

The Lord gave him his answer: 'What hypocrites you are!' he said. 'Is there a single one of you who does not loose his ox or his donkey from the manger and take it out to water on the Sabbath? And here is this woman, a daughter of Abraham, who has been kept prisoner by Satan for eighteen long years: was it wrong for her to be freed from her bonds on the Sabbath?'

(Luke 13.15-16)

Heavenly Lord, the creator of our human minds and bodies, we rejoice that Jesus revealed to us your love in his healing of the sick;
but we rejoice even more that he saw sickness as an evil to be fought, and not as the will of God to be accepted for ever.
May we have the commitment to heal.
May we do our part to make healthy homes.
May we encourage the doctors and nurses who offer their skills that sickness may be defeated.
We pray for those who work today in our hospitals, and those who study in our universities, that they may share in your healing mission.
So, Lord, may your will be done,
and those imprisoned by sickness set free.   Amen

A prayer when I am sick
Today, Father, I feel so useless.
My body is weak,
and pain pierces me.
You know what it is like;
so touch me, Father, hold me,
strengthen me, and give me a new day.

Intercession for medical missionaries
We pray for all who demonstrate your love in their care of the sick;
in distant clinic far from help,
in city slum and crowded maternity ward,
in heat, dust, distress.
Speak through them all, as you spoke through Jesus Christ.

                                     Amen

You may perceive that I understand the secret of Christ. In former generations this was not disclosed to the human race; but now it has been revealed by inspiration to his dedicated apostles and prophets, that through the Gospel the Gentiles are joint heirs with the Jews, part of the same body, sharers together in the promise made in Christ Jesus.   (*Ephesians 3.4-6*)

What a wonderful experience they had, Lord,
in those first days of the Church!
It was a shattering discovery,
that you have no favourites,
and that all may come to your presence
in and through the Lord, Jesus Christ.
May we know this joy, as we meet people
of all colours and languages, and discover
that you make us one family.

Lord, open out our heart and mind
    to glimpse what still the Church could be —
    a source of hope and unity,
a prototype for all mankind.
Help us to honour, trust and serve
    each unknown friend that Christ has made.
    Give us a hope that does not fade,
to build a world of peace and love.   *Brian Wren*

But our gratitude and our hope is wider than the Church. We know that the peace of the world often depends on people with different faiths living in harmony.

Gracious God, you give the spirit of fellowship,
so we thank you for places of reconciliation,
for seeds of hope where people are torn apart.
May we all learn to love our neighbours,
and to work with them, so that in our complex world
we may create something good and constructive.   Amen

> *When they are diminished and brought low*
> *through oppression, trouble, and sorrow,*
> *he pours contempt upon princes*
> *and makes them wander in trackless wastes;*
> *but he raises up the needy out of affliction,*
> *and makes their families like flocks.*
> *Let men consider the steadfast love of the Lord.*
> *(Psalm 107.39-41,43, RSV)*

Each day the heat bears down and the dust rises,
each day the routine is repeated,
and the food we eat seems less and the loneliness worse.
Each day we ask the same question,
Who cares for us? And who can release us?

Dear God, what a mess we have made of your world, for always
we see one group set against another and oppression is like the
chorus in the human tragedy.
We confess our part in this —
    silence, when we are too ignorant or too fearful to speak out,
    selfishness, when we pretend that all is well because we want to
        keep our comfort,
    resignation, when we say that nothing can be done.
We ask for forgiveness. Change these sins within us, so that we
may share in your saving work.

Pray for oppressed people in all parts of the world
May they find that particular freedom
which is their deepest need,
and the life abundant
which is the promise of Christ.

Pray for those who persist in oppression
May they learn that people are indeed people,
not tools, not slaves, not work units,
but brothers and sisters, children of one Father,
your loved ones.

The first gifts brought to Jesus were gold, frankincense and myrrh. Later we read of the gift of loaves and fishes, oil of spikenard, a Passover room, a tomb. People gave what they had. This reminds us of the calls to offer all our human gifts to God, that he may use them as part of the story which is Good News.

Gracious Father, we rejoice in the multitude of gifts found throughout the human family, and we pray that all may be offered for your good purpose.
    We thank you for languages,
        the way of identity and thought;
        and for all who use language with skill.
    We thank you for music and dancing
        which for many is language without words,
        expressing the deepest feelings.
    We thank you for designers and builders
        who, in every part of the world,
        make the surroundings of daily life.
    We thank you for gifts of leadership,
        so varied in every culture,
        so hopeful yet prone to temptation.
    We thank you for gifts of patience and tolerance,
        good humour under stress,
        steadfastness in hardship and neighbourly care,
        for in these we see hope for humanity.
Gracious Father, may such gifts be used, not hidden, that every nation, in its own way, might sing your praise.

O Lord, often I feel that I have nothing to give;
I am drained of enthusiasm,
I lose confidence in my ability and insight.
Then, Lord, show me the richness of creation,
and your joy in what ordinary people can do.
Bless the work of my hands,
through Jesus Christ.

For, lo, he that formeth the mountains, and createth the wind,
and declareth unto man what is his thought, that maketh the
morning darkness, and treadeth upon the high places of the earth,
The Lord, The God of Hosts is his name.

(Amos 4.13, AV)

> Father, we rejoice in the living world;
> we are surprised every day by its beauty,
> its complexity, its mystery.
> May we respect the world of nature,
> knowing that it is your good creation.
> Lift up our hearts as we lift up our eyes
> to clouds, stars, rain, leaves, birds,
> and let us live in thankfulness.

Yet our delight in nature so readily leads us into folly. We can
come to love pets more than people, to claim that we see God in a
sunset but not in our neighbours, to declare that a flower speaks
more than a sermon. And then we start to run away from Christ
and the challenge of the cross.

> Father, I love the beauty of the movement
> in all natural things:
> the flowing stream, the dappled shadows of trees,
> the smooth veins of colour in a pebble,
> the quick delicacy of a kitten.
> But help me to love them aright.
> May I see all the glory of nature
> as the backcloth of the stage,
> with people always most important,
> with your Christ in the midst,
> and your word speaking clearly through him.

A prayer for farm workers
Heavenly Lord, we thank you for all who grow our food. May they
be wise as they use this precious earth and thoughtful as they
harvest its produce, that our children may have good food to eat
and a world still fruitful.   Amen

New every morning is the love
Our wakening and uprising prove;
Through sleep and darkness safely brought,
Restored to life and power and thought.

New mercies, each returning day,
Hover around us while we pray;
New perils past, new sins forgiven,
New thoughts of God, new hopes of heaven.

John Keble

Lord God, this is your day;
you created the sun, our light and energy;
you give sleep as the renewal our minds and bodies need;
each day you are the same God,
always seeking the lost and wounded sheep,
always speaking the creative word for each one.
Help me to enter this day with you.
May I begin to understand your presence
in the events and people who come close to me today.

A prayer for those who wake to a day of drudgery
Lord Jesus, maker of yokes that fit,
I bring to you people I know
who are imprisoned and made bitter
by the hard loads they have to carry today.
May they have friends who will share burdens,
may they be given a patient spirit,
and the daily strength they need.
You, Lord Jesus, are close to them,
you know all about carrying heavy loads,
yours is the cross. Amen

Give thanks for those who worked through the night, remembering
especially —
doctors and nurses in hospitals,
bakers and milkmen,
police and firemen,
train crews and plane crews,
postal sorters and telephone operators,
those who produce our morning papers.
Thank God for all work well done that we might rest in the night.

24

The day is past and over;
All thanks, O Lord, to thee.

For some, evening means release —
    from hard toil or utter concentration,
    from awkward colleagues or daytime heat.
        Lord, grant good rest to them.

For some, evening means satisfaction,
    with a job properly completed
    or a journey made in safety
    or a friendship kept fresh.
        Lord, may tomorrow also be your day.

For some, evening means home and family,
    when children's voices are heard
    and the meal table brings fellowship.
        Lord, hold families together in your love.

For some, evening means excitement,
    when it brings the chance of entertainment,
    going to a party, having an evening out.
        Lord, may pleasure truly refresh and delight.

For others, evening means peace,
    when the telephone stops ringing
    and the shouting world is hushed
    and there is time to remember and think.
        Lord, in quietness and confidence is our strength.

Look back over the day
Dear God, you are always surprising me.
My day was just a few hours of life,
yet in it you were teaching me new things.
You showed me a fresh aspect of familiar people I met,
and new truth about myself.
Forgive my slowness to understand your word;
don't add up the wasted minutes;
judge all my work with a father's mercy.
Thank you, Lord, for the light and the night;
enable me to find renewal in sleep,
and let me know, deep in my heart,
that tomorrow I will be with you, through Jesus Christ.

Read Psalm 69, especially verses 29-36.

It's very quiet, Lord.
The neighbours are all asleep
and there's not much traffic about.
The day's work is behind me and the stars are out.
But I am here with my worry,
my private store of fear,
my nagging frustration, my guilt,
and I cannot rest.

Lord Jesus, you were awake in the garden
when the others were asleep,
and you were in agony, and you prayed.
So I pray.

I don't expect miracles,
like a sudden wiping away of all that is wrong.
I don't know what to expect.
But if you made the stars out there,
if you made the earth to spin,
and the creatures to live,
if when you walked this dusty earth
and bled and suffered
you showed us the eternal God —
then there must be hope at midnight,
for God is in each moment,
never far away, never careless, never asleep.
So let me sleep, and give me strength,
and be with me tomorrow, Lord Jesus.

*Pray for lonely people; for exiles and refugees, for those who have
lost dear friends, and all for whom the darkness of this time seems
to blot out the light of Christ.*

God has gone up with shouts of acclamation,
*   the Lord has gone up with a fanfare of trumpets.*
Praise God, praise him with psalms;
praise our king, praise him with psalms.
God is king of all the earth.   *(Psalm 47.5-7)*

Where can I see this victory, Lord?
When I look at the state of the world today I see holiness and love
defeated very often, and men choosing violence, the way of Cain.
When I look at my own country I see so many empty churches, so
many people turning away from faith, ignorant of Christ.
And when I think of myself, I know how easily my feet turn aside
from the way of Christ.
Can I be confident that God is King of all the earth?

Lord, your victory comes through pain and loss, through total
commitment to the way of love, through cross and tomb.
Give me the grace to see signs of your victory, gospel signs,
pointing to Christ, this very day.

Thanksgiving for the greatness of God's purpose
Gracious God, we understand only a tiny part of the salvation you
are bringing to all the earth.
From the very dawn of life,
through all the ages of human history,
and into distant centuries,
you are the same God.
We wonder, worship and adore, through Christ.

He sent his Son with power to save
From guilt and darkness and the grave:
Wonders of grace to God belong,
Repeat his mercies in your song.   *Isaac Watts*

One experience that we all share is the dependent state of being a child. We look back on this with various emotions, reflecting the attitudes of our parents to us and the style of society in which we lived. Even if there is a dark side to our memories, we recall that 'you, bad as you are, know how to give your children what is good for them'. At the start of life there is a sharing of love.

Heavenly Father, how gracious you are!
In the weakness of babies,
in their inability to look after themselves,
you call forth loving care.
We are thankful for all that our parents
did for us when we could make no return.
Help us to know what are the good gifts
we can share today with little children.

Heavenly Father, how wise you are!
In the expanding world of children,
in their joy of discovery, their expectation,
you are leading them into knowledge of themselves.
We are thankful for the teachers
who stimulated us to explore your complex world.
Help us to share great things in small ways
and eternal hopes in daily deeds.

A prayer for broken homes
You know how often our love for each other breaks down, Lord,
and is replaced by irritation, boredom, dislike and even violence.
Help us to pick up the pieces, to learn the way of forgiveness, and
to know that you are the God of new beginnings.
Give grace and courage to those broken in spirit; help the church
everywhere to minister to them so that life may once again have a
taste of joy.
We ask this through Jesus Christ, our Lord.

*Praise God for everything that brings beauty into human life.
Although passionate love may corrupt, it may also lift human life
above the clay, and touch our hearts with a fire of total self-
offering.*

Father, how wonderful it is to see
two young people absorbed in their love,
devoted to each other, totally at one,
dreaming of life together, and seeing in each other
everything that is good.
It's a miracle how love like that
comes even to the drabbest places
and the most unlikely people.
It's a miracle, Lord, that life is so rich.
So I pray that young lovers may bring their joy
into the life of others.
May they face sorrows together in love;
May they grow old in love.
May your Spirit dwell in their hearts,
that their love may reflect yours, for Christ's sake.

Love and single people
We remember that many live without that experience — through
choice or through accident or through the call of another duty.

Lord God, you call each of us individually, and you have a good
purpose for each one.
May there be fulfilment for those who walk through life alone;
may there always be an open heart to other people, and a new
community in which single people receive wise companions for
their journey.   Amen

Jesus said, 'If you dwell within the revelation I have brought, you are indeed my disciples; you shall know the truth, and the truth will set you free.'

(*John 8.31-32*)

Very easily our love turns to possessiveness, binding people to us and imposing our will. So we pray for that love which liberates.

Lord, we find it easy to bind others,
to set limits, to impose our thinking when we can.
Teach us today that love means letting go —
   so that children may find their own way
   and adults may be themselves;
so may we share in real growth towards maturity.

Lord, it is the same with nations and churches,
so often hoping to be imitated, to have followers,
to turn people into sheep.
Strengthen, we pray, all who struggle for the dignity
of the defenceless, and the freedom of the captives.
May churches everywhere develop their own gifts
and so praise you in every language.
May we see an end to empire-building
in politics and in Christian mission.
We pray this believing that your love
comes into the world to set us free.   Amen

There is often pain in letting go.
Gracious God, you know how hard it is for me
to let go, and so be on my own.
I like to hold close whatever I love.
But you created us in love and you let us go,
although we often turn our backs on you.
Because that is the way of life, help me today
to follow, in confidence and hope,
your kind of love.

Yet on himself he bore our sufferings,
our torments he endured,
while we counted him smitten by God;
struck down by disease and misery;
but he was pierced for our transgressions,
tortured for our iniquities;
the chastisement he bore is health for us
and by his scourging we are healed.

(Isaiah 53.4-5)

Christians cannot read of that sufferer in Isaiah
without thinking of the love of God in Jesus Christ.
The cross he bore is life and health,
Though shame and death to him;
His people's hope, his people's wealth,
Their everlasting theme.   *Thomas Kelly*

Praise be to you, burden-bearing God!
You carry the unending burden of human sin
and still you love us;
You bear the load of struggling humanity
and still you speak the word of life;
You carry the shame of divided and lazy Christians
and still you call us to your feast;
may your love renew us all.

Praise be to you, cross-bearing Jesus!
You carry the burden of the traitor, the coward,
the faithless friends and the slippery crowd.
You carry the load of the penitent thief,
the puzzled administrator and the hard soldiers.
Take my burdens too.
Keep me in your company and teach me how to live.   Amen

Pray for those who carry a heavy burden of personal care for the
elderly or the sick; that they may have patience and skill today.

•

You who once were far off have been brought near in the blood of Christ. For he is our peace, who has made us both one, and has broken down the dividing wall of hostility.

(Ephesians 2.13-14, RSV)

We confess that sin in the world and in us creates dividing walls of hostility.
Heavenly Father, we have been clever in dividing the world into 'us' and 'them':
  rich and poor, black and white,
  old and young, men and women,
  communist and capitalist,
  powerful and powerless,
  people who speak our language
  and those who don't.
The dividing walls are built in our hearts and in our social institutions and habits in order that we may defend ourselves.
So we confess, Father, that we cling to our dividing walls. Change us. Forgive us.

We give thanks for all who share with Christ in breaking down the walls,
  for young people who are open to other cultures and languages;
  for migrants who patiently learn to make a new country their true home;
  for minority groups and their leaders who refuse to shelter behind walls but courageously mix in a tough world;
  for patient teachers in schools where races and cultures meet;
  for politicians who refuse to seek cheap votes but stand firmly for the isolated few;
for all these we thank you, Lord, and ask your grace.

Today I commit myself to being with Christ as he breaks down the walls.
Help me to be open to others, sensitive to their burdens, and ready to pay the price of loving, in the name of Christ our Lord.

My children, love must not be a matter of words or talk; it must be genuine, and show itself in action. This is how we may know that we belong to the realm of truth.   *(1 John 3.18-19)*

Lord, the Church is a mystery, for in every land and through every century, despite our sin, it hands on the life-giving message of grace.
     Thank you, Lord of the Church.
Knowing our own weakness, and our frequent feeling of impatience, you still draw us to the table of your love.
     Thank you, Lord of the Church.
But as we are part of it, so we help to make the Church what it is. We are elements in the ineffectiveness of the Church, and its habitual self-concern.
     Forgive us, Lord of the Church.
We like the rules and the fuss over trifles; we are content to keep the Church to an hour on Sunday, so that our lives are not upset.
     Forgive us, Lord of the Church
So we pray that, as the Church is the community where love and truth come together,
          we may grow in love,
          overcoming all the obstacles of our
          prejudices and facile judgements;
          we may grow in truth,
          until we know the breadth of
          your saving purpose.
You made the Church through your great act in Jesus Christ. Through him you said to us,
     Come, follow me, receive the Spirit.

Grant to the Church everywhere your encouragement, that our love may be genuine and show itself in action.

I believe that the specific task of the church in the modern world, is the Christian celebration of the experience of change. In order to fulfil this task the church will have to renounce progressively the 'power to do good' she now has, and see this power pass into the hands of a new type of institution.　　　*Ivan D. Illich*

Secularisation, though it is a human action, represents the objective reality, the new era in which we find ourselves. It happens to us. We are uprooted from traditional sources of meaning and value. As John the Baptist said, 'The axe is laid to the root of the tree.'　　　*Harvey Cox*

Lord God of every place and time,
we are often lost in nostalgia.
We think that life in the past was simple,
that communities were more friendly,
and earning a living more straightforward.
Help us to recover from that backward look
and face the new realities of our neighbourhood,
the mixture of races, cultures and faiths,
the mobility of young people;
and to see right there opportunity and hope.
Enable us to create new communities
where mutual respect and support
give evidence of your gift of love.　　Amen

We give thanks for the practical forms of love
which we see in our locality.
For courtesy which gets no reward,
for faithfulness in dreary but essential tasks,
for cheerfulness when burdens are heavy,
for care towards the lonely and the sick,
　　we praise you, God our Father.

> *Lord, thou hast been our refuge*
> *from generation to generation.*
> *Before the mountains were brought forth,*
> *or earth and world were born in travail,*
> *from age to age everlasting thou art God.*
>
> *(Psalm 90.1-2)*

O God, how patient you are!
  You make a world that develops over millions of years,
  slowly evolving new forms of life,
  and still in growth today.
  How long you wait for the appearing of the children of light.
  You sent Jesus to us and men killed him.
  We still disobey his word,
  wander far from his clear path,
  ignore his great promises,
  and tiptoe nervously into his new world.

O God, how patient you are!
  Your love for us goes on and on,
  never throwing us aside as worthless,
  always seeing what good may come out of evil.
  Help me to be more like that.
  May I stop prodding other people as though I were the shepherd
    and they the sheep.
  May I set my heart on great things and follow them steadily all
    my days.

O God, be patient still!
  The progress we make in this world is often two steps forward
    and then three steps back again.
  Do not let us go,
  but help us to grow,
  through every experience,
  towards your kingdom.   Amen

The Bible teaches us a concern for justice, which is love translated into social order. Here is one ancient command:

When an alien settles with you in your land, you shall not oppress him. He shall be treated as a native born among you, and you shall love him as a man like yourself, because you were aliens in Egypt. I am the Lord your God.   (*Leviticus 19.33-34*)

O Lord, your word is clear and unambiguous.
You show us that justice for the refugee, the immigrant, the prisoner, the needy, the helpless, is part of the meaning of your kindgom.
    Help us to be courageous in seeking it.
Your command has no limits, Lord;
you give us neighbours to love,
and they are everywhere in this small world.
Justice means fair dealing between nations,
the people we touch in our trade and politics.
    Help us to seek justice far and wide.
Your command has no limits, Lord;
as love continues to the cross,
so justice questions our ancient customs,
and the deepest attitudes of our hearts.
    Help us to open our lives to your word.

Lord God, the injustice in the world frightens us.
We see it in every continent, in powerful groups and in the bitter people who live for violence.
We pray for all who are able to make changes, that they may have respect for all men and women, and wisdom to plan a better future.
    Lord, hear our prayer
    and let our cry come to you.

The first step to wisdom is the fear of the Lord,
* and knowledge of the Holy One is understanding.*
                                                    (Proverbs 9.10)

Jesus knew men so well, all of them, that he needed no evidence
from others about a man, for he himself could tell what was in a
man.   *(John 2.25)*

Now we see only puzzling reflections in a mirror, but then we shall
see face to face.   *(1 Corinthians 13.12)*

Father, we need to confess our lack of understanding.
We see the outside of people and judge them
too easily by their looks and their words.
We classify people by labels;
if they don't agree with us, we are quick to condemn,
and when we are tired and ill at ease
we fail to hear what others are really saying.
Teach us that there are no short cuts
to understanding another person.   Amen

Lord, be merciful, for you know me altogether.
You know how much has to be forgiven.
Your love is great enough for that.   Alleluia!

Thank you, good and gracious Father, for wise people;
for the elderly who reflect on long experience
and so use the past to help shape the future;
for great teachers who see deeply into your purpose;
and for simple people who know
how to receive each day as a miracle.

We pray for understanding between nations
and races and languages.
Where misunderstanding is so very easy,
Lord, teach us in patience your way of love.

So faith, hope, love abide, these three; but the greatest of these is love. (*1 Corinthians 13.13, RSV*)

To us, the greatest demonstration of God's love for us has been his sending his only Son into the world to give us life through him. If God loved us as much as that, surely we, in our turn, should love each other! (*1 John 4.9,11, JBP*)

Father, all-loving and ever-present, I am lost in amazement at your love. When you come closest to me and I glimpse your purpose then I know that justice and punishment, discipline and testing, are not at the centre, but only love. For this I would be thankful every minute of this day and for ever.   Amen

Great God, we know your presence in Jesus Christ
who is one with you for all eternity;
we know your presence in the Holy Spirit
who draws us towards your holiness.
Beyond that is a mystery,
for we can only see in a mirror dimly.
But we trust you because you have come to us
in these ways of power and love.
Keep speaking to us, God, and help us to listen.

Pray for those to whom God is only
— a philosophical idea,
— a word for swearing
— a useful person to blame for accidents
— an authoritarian lawgiver
— a fiction.

Our prayer is, Lord, that all these our brothers and sisters may find at the centre of their lives the great miracle, your grace, which is sufficient for all the needs and longings of your children; through Jesus Christ.   Amen

GOD AND OURSELVES

What do I want?   **Day 1**

> *Praise the Lord, my soul!*
>   *All my being, praise his holy name!*
> *Praise the Lord, my soul,*
>   *and do not forget how kind he is.*
> (*Psalm 103.1-2, GNB*)

The invitation of Jesus: 'Come to me, all of you who are tired from carrying heavy loads, and I will give you rest.'
(*Matthew 11.28, GNB*)

Lord, I give you thanks that in you my deepest needs can be met. Help me to sort out myself and my wants. All my life I seem to have been wanting something: attention, toys, success, beautiful and interesting things. I confess that I have even tried to use people as though they were things; that I have often wanted to say of things: 'These are *mine,* to use as I like.'

The voice of the Master: 'Guard yourselves from every kind of greed; because a person's true life is not made up of the things he *owns,* no matter how rich he may be.'   (*Luke 12.15, GNB*)

When I am at my worst I want my own way. I have wanted to choose for myself what I did; make my own decisions; *do* as I like.

The words of Jesus in Gethsemane: 'My Father! All things are possible for you. Take this cup of suffering away from me. Yet not what I want, but what you want.'   (*Mark 14.36, GNB*)

For me, the hardest thing has always been to answer the question: What do I want to *be?* Not, do I want to be a teacher or a secretary or a politician, but, what sort of person do I want to be?

Lord, keep me from being greedy today; keep me from doing just as I like without asking what you want me to do; show me how to be my true self — the one you want me to be. Give me true peace of heart through inner balance, humility and grace. Let me have your presence every moment and in all I do.

God can held only those who admit their need.

'Tis me, 'tis me, O Lord, standing in the need of prayer.

Socrates once said: 'How many things there are that I don't *want'*. As we go along the Christian pilgrimage we learn how many things there are that we do not *need*. What do I really need?

  To be truly sorry for wrongs I have done, and to know for certain that I am forgiven.

  To have the presence of God in my heart and so to be at peace.

  To have a heart to praise my God, a heart from sin set free.

Lord, grant that I may always have something worth believing, someone worth loving and someone to love me, and something worth doing. Help me to know that I can travel through this mortal life only by the way of grace and forgiveness.

Lord I need your comfort when I am depressed,

  your strength when I have to face suffering,

  your mercy when I go astray,

and at all times the grace of your Holy Spirit to guide me in perplexity and to refresh my soul.

  O Saviour, I have nought to plead,
    In earth beneath or heaven above,
  But just my own exceeding need,
    And thy exceeding love.

  The need will soon be past and gone,
    Exceeding great, but quickly o'er;
  The love unbought is all thine own,
    And lasts for evermore. *Jane Crewsdon*

O God, I thank you that you not only show me what I really need, but also how to find it.

O God, I thank you that you have not promised me freedom from affliction and buffeting by the tempests of this life, but that I shall not be overcome.

> *If I lift up my eyes to the hills,*
> *where shall I find help?*
> *Help comes only from the Lord,*
> *maker of heaven and earth.* (*Psalm 121.1-2*)

O Lord, I need your help to cope with the pressures, temptations, and troubles that will come to me today; to bear the pain, disappointments, strain and stress that I may have to face; to find forgiveness for my sins.

Show me that your help can come to me —

From the Bible: Often in the darkness of fear and doubt a light has shone from your Word upon my path: may that lamp guide my feet this day;

in the darkness of sorrow may your bright beams shine upon me;

in the night of my perversity and wilful blindness, show me your will and how I may fulfil it,

so that in all things I may show your light to others.

From the company of your people: Often your word of rebuke, of comfort, of enlightenment and cheer has come to me in the fellowship of your people;

in the sure knowledge that I belong to that great company, may I this day find the peace that passes all understanding,

and show your love to others.

Through meditation in your presence: Often in the quiet of my heart you have assured me of your care for me;

may nothing, prosperity or adversity, joy or sorrow, this day move me from the certainty of your loving care;

in my defence be a strong tower, in trouble an ever-present comfort, in distress my deliverance,

and in all things give me power to show your loving care to others.

O Lord, give me this day the help I need to face its demands and fulfil my duties.

> *How shall I sing that majesty*
> *Which angels do admire?*
> *Let dust in dust and silence lie;*
> *Sing, sing, ye heavenly choir.*
> *Thousands of thousands stand around*
> *Thy throne, O God most high;*
> *Ten thousand times ten thousand sound*
> *Thy praise; but who am I?*   *John Mason*

Lord, I am a sinner; in daily need of that cleansing and forgiveness that come alone from you.

Deliver me this day from selfish desires; from the power and guilt of pride and sin, so that I may serve you with a free spirit.

Lord, I am a beggar; and the alms I crave is a gift from you.

Give me, this day, I pray, a will that is loyal to your commands; a heart that is at rest in your love, and a mind that is governed by your discipline, so that seeing you at work in your world and in my life, I may bless you for what you withhold from me as well as for what you provide.

Lord, I am your child, as well as your servant.

For the unspeakable privilege of being taught by Jesus to call you my Father in heaven, I thank you, Lord.

As a little child owes everything to loving parents, I owe all I have to you.

Here is the foundation of my hope and confidence. Under the shelter of your wings I shall find peace this and every day.

May I carry about with me the infection of a good courage.

I am me

In all the wonder of your creation, the sheer mystery of being, and the power that sustains the whole universe, the most amazing thing to me is my own existence, my awareness of myself and, through that, my awareness of your presence in everything and at all times.

Father, help me to live this day as in the light of eternity and with the certainty that you are with me.

O come, let us worship and bow down: let us kneel before the
Lord our maker.   (*Psalm 95.6, AV*)

> *Thy hands created me, thy hands*
> *From sin have set me free,*
> *The mercy that hath loosed my bands*
> *Hath bound me fast to thee.*   *Charles Wesley*

Contemplate the majesty of God as revealed in his creation
From his hands came the elements: wind and rain, thunder and
sunshine; mountain and ocean. He sustains all life upon the
earth. Seed time and harvest, germination, growth and decay, are
all part of his great plan.

What does it mean to realise that, along with the whole creation,
we come from the hands of God?
>   It means that we acknowledge our total dependence on him for
>   every good and perfect gift.
>   For the medieval mystic Juliana of Norwich it meant that we
>   are cut down to size: 'It is the loving contemplation of its
>   Maker that causes the soul to realise its own insignificance.'
>   For Jesus it meant that we must serve our fellows in humility:
>   Jesus, well aware that he had come from God and was going
>   back to God ... began to wash his disciples' feet.

What does it mean to realise that my family, my friends, my
neighbours, my colleagues, — all those I meet day by day — also
come from his hands?
>   Lord, it means that I can never despise any one of your
>   children;
>   that they, too, are made in your image and bear upon their
>   brow the mark of the eternal;
>   that every human relationship can be blessed by you and
>   become a source of blessing.

O God, may I this day
>   so contemplate your power and goodness that I may learn true
>   humility and realise my own insignificance;
>   so recollect that all I have and all I am come by mercy and
>   grace from your hands that my hands may be dedicated in
>   service for you and my fellows.

Fill thou my life, O Lord my God,
   In every part with praise,
That my whole being may proclaim
   Thy being and thy ways.

Praise in the common things of life,
   Its goings out and in;
Praise in each duty and each deed,
   However small and mean.   *Horatius Bonar*

Two things are sure:
   I came not to this place by chance.
   I was not brought into the world to do just as I like, but to fulfil the plan which God has for me.

God's purpose in the cross was to bring us out of the futility of meaningless existence, to redeem us. He comes to us with the question, 'What are you doing with your life? Are you drifting at the mercy of every wind of thought and rumour? Or have you a foundation laid upon a rock?'

In answering these questions we find we must ask God —
   to teach us how to ask aright for his blessings;
   to be our guide in the confusion of our life;
   to draw us ever closer to himself until at the end we stand in his
     immediate and glorious presence;
   to find joy in all that is good and true, and satisfaction in
     serving others.

Lord, it is my chief delight to go along the path that you have chosen for me, just as Jesus walked along a chosen way, steadfast in faith, meek of spirit, and with the gentleness of love. Outward events so easily scatter my thoughts, disturb my inner peace, and deflect me from the right path, that I pray for your spirit to calm my soul, settle the tumult inside me and subdue my thoughts into captivity to yourself. Do not let the cares and duties of this life press so heavily upon me this day that I lose the sense of your guidance. Enable me to follow your path with a quiet and thankful heart so that I may offer you acceptable service.

Captain of Israel's host, and guide
  Of all who seek the land above,
Beneath thy shadow we abide,
  The cloud of thy protecting love;
Our strength, thy grace; our rule, thy word;
Our end, the glory of the Lord.

By thine unerring Spirit led,
  We shall not in the desert stray;
We shall not full direction need,
  Nor miss our providential way;
As far from danger as from fear,
While love, almighty love, is near.   *Charles Wesley*

The Christian life is a pilgrimage
It is a journey that brings us to a holy place:
  Heavenly Father, show me the way to the Holy City where you
  dwell and where I shall be fully aware of your presence. Cleanse
  my heart that I may be prepared to meet you face to face. Keep
  me from ever losing a sense of awe as I draw nearer to the
  heavenly Jerusalem.
It takes us by an unknown way:
  Lord Jesus, I know that the path will often be rough. But you
  have been this way before me, and I have already found that
  you are with me when the going is hard. I have no idea what lies
  ahead; what will be asked of me, or where you will ask me to
  go; I only know that I can never be beyond your love and care.
  You will be with me all the way.
It is a journey that can only begin from where we are, and we can
only see a short distance ahead:
  Lead, kindly light, amid the encircling gloom
    Lead thou me on!
  The night is dark, and I am far from home;
    Lead thou me on!
  Keep thou my feet; I do not ask to see
  The distant scene: one step enough for me.   *J.H. Newman*

Grant, heavenly Father, that this day I may keep to the path of
my pilgrimage so that, when night comes and my work is done, I
may know that I have pitched my moving tent a day's march
nearer home.

Lord God, creator of the universe, you who care for all your children; I praise you for your wisdom and power which are beyond my thought, and trust you for your infinite goodness and love which support me every day of my life. And I offer my thanksgiving for all the things you ask me to do. Make me more worthy to serve you and more willing to do your will.

Lord, let me not live to be useless. *John Wesley*

I can determine that whatever I may do this day will be done in the name of Jesus and to the glory of God
Lord, I acknowledge that this means:
   nothing mean or shoddy or unworthy can enter into my work;
   only those things which are in line with your will can be offered to you;
   that when I have done my best I can leave to you the outcome and result.

I can be quiet in the presence of God
Lord, this means that:
   you will take from my soul all sense of strain or stress, all useless fuss;
   there will be order and economy in all I do, rather than confusion and wasted time or energy;
   I shall find time for prayer, and praise, and gratitude for your infinite goodness.

I can be myself, not attempting to present a mask, a facade, to those I meet. This means that:
   it is no longer I who live but Christ who lives within me;
   I shall truly discover what it means to be a child of God, made in his own image;
   there will be no place for personal aggression or the wrong kind of pride in anything I do.

I can think more of others than about myself, serving and loving them in the name of Jesus.

O Lord, help me this day to keep a quiet place in my heart where you can speak to me. Give me that peace which the world cannot give, so that stayed in thy tranquillity I may do all things to your glory.

I fall on my knees before the Father, from whom every family in heaven and on earth receives its true name.

(Ephesians 3.14-15, GNB)

> *How do thy mercies close me round!*
> *For ever be thy name adored!*
> *I blush in all things to abound;*
> *The servant is above his Lord!*   Charles Wesley

Father, I thank you that you have given me the immense blessing of being a member of two families. In the loving world of the home I am —
    loved for who I am, not for what I own;
    understood, and my failings are forgiven;
    treated with respect, but my pride is punctured;
    comforted when defenceless from outside attacks;
    healed when hurt, lifted up when cast down;
    rebuked when I am at fault, and guided when I am perplexed.

Father of every family on earth, I am grateful for —
    laughter that refreshes;
    frank speech that releases tension;
    love which has no favourites;
    the confidence each member has in the integrity and loyalty of
        others;
    the sympathy which truly feels for the others;
    the companionship the family provides;
    your great family, the Church.

I pray that I may be a good member of my families — home and church. Make me sensitive to the needs and moods of others;
              slow to meet criticism with resentment;
              swift to forgive injury — real or imagined;
              ready to give comfort to others;
              gentle in offering advice;
              always willing to help.

Pray by name for members of your two families — home and church — in their special needs.

Self-examination: Is there anything I should do today for a member of my home or church? Am I so concerned with those families as to be too much turned-in and forgetful of my duty to others?

*I bless the holy name of God with all my heart. Yes, I will bless
the Lord and not forget the glorious things he does for me.*
(*Psalm 103.1-2, LB*)

The most needy are our neighbours if we notice well.
Piers Plowman
Forgive us that so little of thy love has reached others through
us, and that we have borne so lightly wrongs and sufferings that
were not our own. Forgive us wherein we have cherished the
things that divide us from others, and wherein we have made it
hard for them to live with us; And wherein we have been
thoughtless in our judgements, hasty in condemnation,
grudging in forgiveness. (*Methodist Covenant Service*)

Who is my neighbour? Read the story of the Good Samaritan:
Luke 10.25-37.
Forgive me, Lord, that I have had so narrow a concept of
neighbourliness, not only in the little I have done for those who
live close by, but also in my forgetfulness of those who are
brought near to me by the inventions of modern science and
technology. Help me to cope with the compassion that is
aroused in me by events I read about in the papers or see on
television, so that I do not become callous and unresponsive in
the face of the great disasters that take place.

We have a special responsibility for those who live in our neighbourhood.
Remember them by name.

Neighbourliness is based on give and take.
Give thanks for the 'glorious things' that have come from those
who live nearby.

Every task, however simple, sets the soul that does it free;
Every deed of love and mercy done to man, is done to me.
Nevermore thou needest seek me; I am with thee everywhere;
Raise the stone, and thou shalt find me; cleave the wood
and I am there. *Henry Van Dyke*

O Lord, grant that in the common tasks of life we may raise the
stone to build an altar and cleave wood for the daily sacrifice of
our consecrated powers.

*Who is like unto thee, O Lord? Who is like thee, glorious in
holiness, fearful in praises, doing wonders?*
Let old men and children,
  young men and maidens,
  high and low, rich and poor,
  one with another let them praise the name of the Lord.
          (Exodus 15.11, AV; Based on Psalms 148.12-13; 49.2)

One thing I can do for my neighbours is to pray for them regularly
by name.
   Bring your neighbours one by one to God in prayer; mentioning
   their special needs; giving thanks for the grace of friendship
   you have received at their hands.

I can visit my neighbours, especially those who are in trouble; the
old and lonely; the sick and the infirm. I can share in their joys in
times of happiness and let them share in those things wherein
God has blessed me.

I can serve my neighbours, in the name of Jesus, in their times of
need.
   Lord make me open to the moods and condition of others.
   Help me to keep a true balance between intrusion into their
   private affairs and indifference to their troubles.
   Make me readily available, generous in spirit, sufficiently at
   leisure to be able to help when needed.
   From my own experience of being comforted by those who have
   received your comfort, may I learn how to share your
   strength with others.
   Make me alert when there is a cry for help at the deepest level,
   and then, O Lord, give me tact, give me wisdom, give me love.

Lord, you love all men. Your goodness, wisdom, power and love
can save us. As you led our fathers when they called to you, and
helped them in their pilgrimage, so when we come to you in need,
fear, temptation and trouble, deliver us, we beseech you, O Lord.
From all perplexity of mind, loneliness of thought and brooding
in discontent; from evading our responsibility towards our
neighbours and all selfishness of purpose; from all that separates
us from others, good Lord deliver us.

Praise the Lord, O my soul;
  Blessed art thou, O Lord.
O Lord, how manifold are thy works! in widsom hast thou
made them all;
  Blessed art thou, O Lord.
I will sing unto the Lord as long as I live; I will
praise my God while I have my being;
  Blessed art thou, O Lord.
    O my soul, praise the Lord.

Lord, I pray for those I work with: my colleagues, workmates and partners; those I work for and those who work for me. May my relationship with them be such as you can bless: full of compassion, understanding and loyalty. Let me be swift to know when they are in trouble, ready when they need help, friendly to the lonely and able to share in the joys of others.

May our industries, trades and professions have your blessing. May the chief concern of all who labour be for the common good and hasten the day when men and women shall see in the work of hand and brain which they do, a way of serving you, of praising you, of giving you thanks for all the great benefits we have received at your hands. As your Son when he was on earth became a craftsman and mastered the use of tools, give to each of us a sense of pride in work well done and of dignity in supplying the needs of others.

> Son of the carpenter, receive
>   This humble work of mine;
> Worth to my meanest labour give,
>   By joining it to thine.   *Charles Wesley*

Give me sympathy and understanding, Lord, for all who want to work but are unemployed; all who work hard, but find it difficult to make ends meet in providing for family and dependents. And help me this day to go to the bench, the desk, the sink, the counter, the hospital bed or operating table, as to an altar.

To God the Father, who first loved us, and made us accepted in
the Beloved;
To God the Son, who loved us, and washed us from our sins in his
own blood;
To God the Holy Ghost, who sheds the love of God abroad in our
hearts,
Be all love and all glory for time and for eternity
                                                    Bishop Thomas Ken

Lord, I am not worthy to receive so much good from you and at
the hands of men and women. Hear my confession as I
acknowledge my weakness, failure, selfishness, and sin, and
grant me full forgiveness, grant me peace.

I remember before you those known to me who do so much to
make my life possible, bearable, worthwhile and pleasant:
> those who help to supply me with food: the milkman, the
> butcher, and those who serve in the baker's shop;
> those who bring me letters and newspapers.

I give thanks for, and ask your blessing upon, those I see but
fleetingly, who serve me day by day:
> those who drive the trains or buses that take me safely to work
> or recreation;
> those who inform and entertain me on radio and television.

And I pray for the great company, unknown to me by sight or
name, who make it possible for me to receive so many benefits:
> those who grow my food or win it from the sea, and convey it to
> the markets and the shops;
> those who spin thread, weave cloth, manufacture clothes;
> those who provide the services on which I so much depend:
> water, gas, electricity; miners, firemen, coastguards;
> those who sort and convey letters and parcels; print news-
> papers, magazines and books; arrange radio and television
> programmes and provide the technical knowledge which
> puts them on the air;
> policemen, ambulance men, workers in hospitals and clinics
> who care for my safety and health;
> those who teach, and gather knowledge, and make discoveries
> and inventions; who make life more delightful, interesting
> and safe;
> the workers in our heavy industries; our factories, banks and
> shops.

May I humbly make my offering to the common good.

> *We give thanks to you, O God,*
> *we give thanks to you!*
> *We proclaim how great you are*
> *and tell of the wonderful things you have done.*
>
> *(Psalm 75.1, GNB)*

An act of penitence
Father God, I remember with sorrow the many cruel and ruthless things which have been done in the name of my country:

the natural resources that have been exploited,

the people sold into slavery,

the towns destroyed by bombing,

the prisoners held and rulers deposed.

For such acts of violence and greed I beg forgiveness.

An act of honourable remembrance
Almighty God, I thank you that there is much in our national history to recall with justifiable pride. So with joy and dignity I honour:

those who have given themselves to raise the standard of life in other lands;

missionaries who have taught in schools and colleges, doctors and nurses who have risked their own health and lives to bring healing to the sick and comfort to the dying, evangelists who have brought hope and confidence by telling of your love for all mankind;

those government officials and traders who have brought peace, prosperity and hope in place of superstition, cruelty and poverty.

For the great company of those who have shown, by lives of integrity, compassion and dedication, something of your nature to people all over the world, I give you thanks.

An act of petition
Pray for your country and its present needs:

for good relationships with people of other lands and other cultures, especially those living here;

for peace and goodwill in politics, industry, and the social life of the community;

for schools, colleges and hospitals;

for the life of the Church, that it may be a living force for good.

Pray that you may play your part in the nation's life.

The world and all that is in it belong to the Lord; the earth and all who live on it are his. *(Psalm 24.1, GNB)*

Forgive me, Father, that so often I do not live as if I belong to you. Help me to remember that I am a citizen of heaven; looking to you for deliverance, living as a subject under your authority, even though for a while I am in a distant place.

Help me also to remember that I am a citizen of the world; that you made all men of one family throughout all the earth, and in that sense all men are my brothers.

So help me now to pray with understanding, compassion, and a firm reliance on your mercy, for those places in the world where there is bitterness and division, natural disaster, or a moment of decision; giving thanks for those who work for good relationships between the nations, peace and goodwill among all men, and the alleviation of want, ignorance, and suffering. (Where possible, mention such places and people by name.)

Say the Lord's Prayer.

Lord, make us instruments of thy peace.
Where there is hatred, let us sow love;
where there is injury, pardon;
where there is discord, union;
where there is doubt, faith;
where there is despair, hope;
where there is darkness, light;
where there is sadness, joy;
for thy mercy and for thy truth's sake.

St Francis of Assisi

Help me, Lord, this day
   as a member of my family,
   as a good neighbour,
   as a citizen of my country, and
   as a citizen of the world,
to act as a citizen of heaven, doing everything according to your will.

> *I sing the almighty power of God*
> *That made the mountains rise,*
> *That spread the flowing seas abroad,*
> *And built the lofty skies.* Isaac Watts

When I consider your power, Lord, I am bewildered by the thought of the energy that could
  'stretch out the sky like a curtain'
  create a sun pouring out energy that can sunburn us on a beach 93 million miles away;
  create not just one sun, but the 100,000 million suns in our galaxy; not just one galaxy, but all the 100,000 million galaxies in our universe.

When I remember that you created all the sources of energy: oil that powers our cars and aeroplanes; electricity that gives us light and heat and motion; the power of waterfall and thunderstorm, of wind and tide;
I am profoundly grateful that you are a good and loving God;
I am more than ever aware of my own weakness, and in my need I rely more and more upon your strength.

Bring into my life, Lord, the power of your love — the love that is wide enough to embrace the whole world.
Bring that power into those places where I am most defeated, hopeless and defenceless.
Give me the power to do your will, and to help others when they lack resources to face the demands of life.

Help me this day to live in the light of the promises of your word:
When the Holy Spirit comes upon you, you will be filled with power, and you will be witnesses for me. (*Acts 1.8, GNB*)
I have complete confidence in the gospel; it is God's power to save all who believe. (*Romans 1.16, GNB*)
The message about Christ's death on the cross is nonsense to those who are being lost; but for us who are being saved it is God's power. (*1 Corinthians 1.18, GNB*)
Your faith, then, does not rest on human wisdom but on God's power. (*1 Corinthians 2.5, GNB*)

I had fainted, unless I had believed to see the goodness of the
Lord in the land of the living. (*Psalm 27.13, AV*)

> *Faithful, O Lord, thy mercies are,*
>   *A rock that cannot move:*
> *A thousand promises declare*
>   *Thy constancy of love.*
>
> *Throughout the universe it reigns,*
>   *Unalterably sure;*
> *And while the truth of God remains,*
>   *The goodness must endure.* *Charles Wesley*

Meditate upon the enduring goodness of God shown
  in listening to our prayers;
  in caring for the lonely;
  in raising the fallen and the distressed;
  in showing mercy to those who come to him in humble
    penitence, and forgiveness to those who are ready to forgive
    others.

Give thanks to God for
  his loving-kindness which enables us to love those who need our
    encouragement and support;
  every good and perfect gift that has come to us at his hands:
    life; a sense of humour; intelligence to link what comes to us
    through our senses and make a pattern of meaning for our
    existence; friendship; all holy and happy memories, and the
    good things of our physical being: food, and shelter, and
    clothing, and all that lends interest and stimulus to our
    existence.
Above all, give thanks to God for all he has done for us through
Jesus Christ, our Saviour.

As I contemplate the infinite goodness of God,
  I am filled with gratitude that his immense power is used in
    love and mercy;
  I am compelled to examine my heart and find how far I fall
    short of his glory and goodness;
  I review the events, appointments, and duties of the coming
    day, to be in some measure prepared beforehand so that I
    may, in my own life, and by the power of his Holy Spirit,
    show forth his goodness.

> *For the beauty of the earth,*
> *For the beauty of the skies,*
> *For the love which from our birth*
> *Over and around us lies,*
> *Gracious God, to thee we raise*
> *This our sacrifice of praise.*   *F.S. Pierpoint*

Inspire me, O Lord, so that I may see the beauty of your creation: give me the vision of the beauty of holiness; eyes and ears to appreciate the loveliness of earth and sky and stars, the song of birds, the colour of flowers, the movement of animals; a mind to comprehend something of the incredible beauty of the structure of matter, the laws of nature and the unity of all that you have made in this vast universe.
But most of all let me perceive the beauty of your mind in the everlasting gospel, and in the lives of those who have been redeemed by your grace and live in your presence.

Lord, you created light and renew that gift to us every morning, blessing all alike — good and evil — with your sunshine;
shed, I pray, the bright beams of your mercy upon my soul;
illuminate my mind with your truth and make radiant my heart
    with your love;
so that in your light I may see light and recognise, in the beauty of
    the earth, the beauty of its Creator; and at the end may I see
    your perfect beauty and eternal glory.

Show me, Lord, your beauty in the lives of those who have been renewed by the love of Jesus, and grant to me the unspeakable privilege and grace of showing you to others.

Give thanks to God for all the inspiration and insight that have come to us from those who have been most sensitive to beauty: artists, poets, musicians, sculptors, dramatists and architects, and for the awe and wonder their work arouses in us.

Father, in the midst of the beauty and wonder of your creation men have brought ugliness and evil. Forgive us for this desecration, and help me this day by prayer and work to worship you in the beauty of holiness.

God is love.   (*1 John 4.8*)

Lord, teach me what it means to live in the light of the knowledge
that you are pure, unbounded love.
At the beginning of this day, I ask your forgiveness for the ways in
which I have hurt your heart of love.
Though I have done nothing to deserve such love as you have
shown to me in Jesus Christ, yet with confidence I pray that
throughout the coming hours I may be sure of your loving-
kindness surrounding me in all I do, guiding me wherever I may
go.

I give thanks for the comfort of your love for me; for the humility
that springs from being close to you; for the constraints that your
love imposes on my life; for since Christ in his infinite love died
for me, then I can no longer live for myself but only for him. Let
me not turn aside to anything, however profitable, interesting,
desirable, if it be not in complete accordance with your will, the
thing you want me to do.

Shew me that without your love in my heart I can do nothing
worthwhile, but that your love can make me
     patient with others and kind to those I meet;
     never jealous, entirely without conceit or pride;
     never selfish, irritable, petty or rude.
Let me never keep a score of wrongs that others have done against
me, never be pleased by trouble that comes to others, but only
find joy in those things that are good and true and beautiful.

Give me the assurance that nothing can separate me from your
love and that
     trouble cannot take me out of your hands;
     hardship and persecution, poverty and danger cannot divide
         me from you;
     not even death is able to keep us apart.

Today, Father, fill me with your love so that
     I may love others as you love me;
     I may do those things that will be pleasing to you;
     I may go with joy along my pilgrim way.

Jesus, bearing the human likeness, revealed in human shape, humbled himself, and in obedience accepted even death — death on a cross.   (*Part of Philippians 2.5-8*)

An act of humble confession
God, have mercy on me, sinner that I am.
O God, you know me better than I know myself; you see the sin that my sinfulness hides from me; but my conscience reminds me that

    often I am not alert to your presence;
    I do not always act with love to others;
    I am not always humble towards you; willing to give myself to
        you, to be crucified with you, and to share in your work.

Accept this confession; lift up my head; give me hope and healing, grace to go on in the path you have chosen, and joy in your love.

God shows his humility in waiting for us to accept his forgiveness, friendship and love: Behold, I stand at the door, and knock: if any man hear my voice, and open the door, I will come in to him.

An act of faith
Lord God, I believe in your humility because

    I have seen the humility of faithful, Christ-like people;
    you did not send your Son to live with us as a powerful prince in
        a monarch's palace, but as a baby in a lowly cattle-shed;
    your infinite power is not used to invade my personality,
        compelling me in spite of my preferences and desires to go
        your way, but with reticence and respect for me as unique
        and precious.

An act of supplication
Heavenly Father, keep me from that pride which is the fountain-head of all deadly sins; from the arrogance of being more aware of my own opinions and effectiveness, even of my faults and failings, than of the feelings of others and the demands of the situation around me; and from being proud of my own humility. Make me sensitive and approachable, so that I may encourage shy people and hear the call for help from those who find it hard to put their appeal into words.

> *Man lives not for himself alone;*
> *In others' good he finds his own.*
>   *H.C. Shuttleworth*

Recall the nature of our Christian fellowship and ask that you
may share in it fully:

we think and feel the same on the great issues of life and death;
the problems of the community, and the essentials of the
faith;

we share the same love and are one in soul and mind;

we partake of the same loaf and drink from the same cup in the
central act of our fellowship;

we suffer with members who suffer and rejoice with those who
rejoice;

we do nothing aggressively, but are humble towards each other,
always considering others better than ourselves;

we are always on the look-out for the interests of the others and
not just for our own.

Ask forgiveness for the many times you have fallen short of this
high ideal, neglecting fellowship and acting without love.

Lord, help me to show compassion, kindness, humility,
gentleness, and patience, springing out of my fellowship with
your people in the love of Christ and the power of the Holy Spirit;
make me tolerant with others, always ready to forgive because you
have forgiven me;
help me to contribute to the rich fellowship of the Church as well
as to derive strength from it, giving and receiving good.

> In the communion of the saints
>   Is wisdom, safety and delight;
> And, when my heart declines and faints,
>   It's raisèd by their heat and light!   *Richard Baxter*

Lord, I thank you for all the benefits which have come to me
through being a member of your Church: all the love and support
I have received in times of sorrow and depression; all the
friendship and company that have saved me from loneliness; the
restraint that has kept me from doing wrong, and the stimulus to
serve you and my fellows.
Make me, this day, worthy of this high privilege.

> *Arise, Jerusalem,*
> *rise clothed in light; your light has come*
>   *and the glory of the Lord shines over you.*
> *For, though darkness covers the earth*
>   *and dark night the nations,*
>   *the Lord shall shine upon you*
>   *and over you shall his glory appear;*
>   *and the nations shall march towards your light*
>   *and their kings to your sunrise.*   *(Isaiah 60.1-3)*

Father of all mankind, we give you thanks for the great company of those who, having seen the vision of a world redeemed by you through our Lord Jesus Christ, have gone out with the message of your universal love.

Especially we thank you for
  those who brought the good news to our own country;
  the many, some famous, some whose names are forgotten, who
    have shown by their words, and even more by their lives, the
    glory of your love for all people, here and throughout the
    world;
  those who have taught us how to worship; the writers of hymns,
    composers of music, translators of the Bible, and authors of
    prayers, who have made your presence real to ordinary folk,
    and shown us how to live more nearly as we pray, so that our
    work and worship may be one.

Forgive me, Lord, that I have done so little to lighten the darkness over the world; show me how my gifts and experience may be of service to your great purpose of winning all mankind for goodness, truth, and love; and equip me to answer your call no matter how humble, difficult, or important, may be the tasks that you require me to perform.

Help me, Lord, this day to live with the high sense of privilege that comes from knowing myself to be an heir to all the promises of God proclaimed in the scriptures; a member of the great Church which is the body of Christ; a partaker in the world mission of that Church.

O give thanks unto the Lord, for he is good: for his mercy endureth for ever.
O that men would praise the Lord for his goodness, and for his wonderful works to the children of men! (*Psalm 107.1,8, AV*)

Stir up, we beseech thee, O Lord, the wills of thy faithful people; that they, plenteously bringing forth the fruit of good works, may of thee be plenteously rewarded; through Jesus Christ our Lord.
(*Book of Common Prayer*)

The harvest of the Spirit is
    love, joy, peace,
    patience, kindness, goodness,
    fidelity, gentleness, and self-control. (*Galatians 5.22-23*)
And as soon as you start talking like this you have gone beyond the world of common sense.
Lord, help me to see that in some circumstances common sense may be disastrous to live by. Remind me that there was no common sense in
    Mary breaking a box of precious ointment over her Master's
        feet;
    those early missionaries going to face malaria in West Africa or
        cannibals in Fiji;
and, yet, that these are among the imperishable memories of the human race.

Help me, O Lord, to see that goodness, personal sanctity, involves the service of others and that it can never be selfish even in its enjoyment of your friendship;
help me to learn how to take decisions: not to suit my own inclinations, on grounds of expediency, 'safe' considerations, but with the welfare of others in mind and for the common good;
and help me this day to learn a little of what it means to obey your commands: to turn the other cheek; go the second mile; love my enemies; be perfect.
May I become as a little child and so enter into your kingdom.

My tongue shall speak of thy righteousness and of thy praise all the day long.   *(Psalm 35.28, AV)*

The voice of the Master: I assure you that anyone who gives you a drink of water because you belong to me will certainly receive his reward.   *(Mark 9.41, GNB)*
The voice of the disciple: When, Lord, did we ever see you hungry and feed you, or thirsty and give you a drink? When did we ever see you a stranger and welcome you in our homes, or naked and clothe you? When did we ever see you sick or in prison, and visit you?   *(Matthew 25.37-39, GNB)*
The voice of the Master: I tell you, whenever you did this for one of the least important of these brothers of mine you did it for me!
                                                     (Matthew 25.40, GNB)

Christian service is more than social engineering: it is offered in the name of Christ.

Lord, grant that in true humility I may offer service to you by serving others;
help me, without being officious, to share the burdens of my neighbours, making myself available so that in the moment of their need they may know me as their friend, willing and ready to help;
make me loving towards the members of my family, and make me always willing to accept the service which others offer me.

Review the coming day
The duties you may have to fulfil; the demands you may be required to face; the people you are likely to meet.
Ask for God's grace that you may serve others, not out of a sense of superiority or condescension, but in the name of Christ.
Accept the assurance that he will grant you the strength to do his will, and that although in the perplexities and problems which surround you, you may not have peace of mind, yet he will give you peace of heart, tranquillity of spirit.

Forth in thy name, O Lord, I go,
My daily labour to pursue,
Thee, only thee, resolved to know
In all I think, or speak, or do.   *Charles Wesley*

> *Jesus, my strength, my hope,*
> *On thee I cast my care,*
> *With humble confidence look up,*
> *And know thou hear'st my prayer.*
> *Give me on thee to wait,*
> *Till I can all things do,*
> *On thee, almighty to create,*
> *Almighty to renew.*   *Charles Wesley*

> *Depend upon the Lord,*
> *and he will grant you your heart's desire.*   *(Psalm 37.4)*

The promise of God to those who love him is that he will be with them in trouble.

Recall those times when you have been in trouble and God has been with you, renewing your faith;
consider the present difficulties and troubles that you face, for each one recalling with gratitude a blessing with which God has enriched your life;
remember those you know to be in trouble, praying that God's grace may be with each in their special needs.

Lord Jesus Christ, you know what it means to face danger and difficulty; to be threatened by the forces of evil, and to be troubled by the approach of anguish, death, and separation; you know how easily I become afraid; how great is the darkness of depression and misery that sometimes seems to overwhelm me. In all the sorrow, pain, and distress that you have had to face, you never lost your faith in the goodness of your Father; grant that I, too, may go through the difficulties and troubles of this mortal life with a serene confidence that God in his loving-kindness will never leave me nor forsake me.

Say the Lord's Prayer.

> *Son of God, if thy free grace*
> *Again hath raised me up,*
> *Called me still to seek thy face,*
> *And given me back my hope;*
> *Still thy timely help afford,*
> *And all thy loving-kindness show:*
> *Keep me, keep me, gracious Lord,*
> *And never let me go!*   *Charles Wesley*

Truly my soul is silent waiting all hushed upon God.
  O praise God in his holiness.

Worship the Lord in the beauty of holiness!
Bow down before him, his glory proclaim.   *J.S.B. Monsell*

Lord, I know my weakness and sinfulness; my complete unworthiness to be called by your name; forgive, I pray, my disobedience and selfishness and grant to me, even to me, some of the beauty of your holiness.

Recall the obedience of Jesus
Remember his complete devotion to the purpose of God so that it became possible for him to say: 'It is meat and drink for me to do the will of him who sent me until I have finished his work.'

Lord Jesus Christ, give me obedience like yours, so that even when I am faced with a path I fear and dislike to tread, I may say, as you said in the garden of Gethsemane: 'Take this cup of suffering from me. Yet not what I want, but what you want.'

Give me also, I pray, faithfulness, loyalty and obedience, not merely in the supreme, dramatic moments of my life when I am keyed-up to accept whatever in your mercy may be in store for me, but in the little things of everyday life when I find it so much easier to please myself, seek my own comfort, find the easy way. Help me to discover what it means to take upon myself with joy the yoke of obedience.

Almighty God, you created me for your glory and your service — that service which is perfect freedom. Give me grace, I pray, that this day I may hallow every gift and improve every talent which you have committed to me. May I, with a blithe, cheerful, and diligent spirit truly serve you, and may all that I do be done in the Name of Jesus Christ.

When we walk with the Lord
In the light of his word
What a glory he sheds on our way!
While we do his good will,
He abides with us still,
And with all who will trust and obey.
          J.H. Sammis

> *Praise, my soul, the King of heaven;*
>   *To his feet thy tribute bring;*
> *Ransomed, healed, restored, forgiven,*
>   *Who like thee his praise should sing?*
>   *Praise him! Praise him!*
>   *Praise the everlasting King.*   H.F. Lyte

Forgive us our sins,
for we too forgive all who have done us wrong.
                              (Part of the Lord's Prayer: Luke 11.4)

O God, you are the only one to whom I can turn for forgiveness and renewal: you know the secrets of my heart and the outward actions of my everyday life better than I know them myself; for the sins and wrongs and selfish acts which I know that I have committed, grant me full forgiveness and cleansing; for the evil that I am not even aware of, grant me your grace and a new approach to life.

O God, who through your Son, Jesus Christ, has taught us that we may be forgiven only in so far as we have forgiven others the wrongs they have done to us, give me a truly forgiving spirit. However hard it may be, let me go more than half-way to restore broken relationships. Let me forgive, not grudgingly, meanly, holding back, but freely, generously, and graciously, even when I am rejected and my offer is refused.

O God, you are the eternal source of true peace, the tranquillity that comes through perfect goodness;
    your reward to those who love you is the gift of that forgiveness which brings your peace into our hearts;
    you have taught us, by the life and words of your Son, the Prince of peace, that your children are peacemakers and seekers of reconciliation,
    so grant that your peace, which is beyond my utmost understanding, may guard and direct my heart and thoughts this day, through Jesus Christ our Lord.

Blessed be God
the creator, preserver and governor of all things:
whose kingdom is an everlasting kingdom,
and his dominion from generation to generation.
He is the blessed and only Potentate,
King of kings and Lord of lords,
who only hath immortality,
dwelling in the light unapproachable:
and though he hath his dwelling so high,
yet he humbleth himself to behold,
the things that are in heaven and earth.

Lancelot Andrewes

O God, I offer you my humble, grateful thanks that although you are above all earthly splendour in your power and authority, beyond all human thought in your goodness and perfection, yet by your infinite loving-kindness and gracious love I can come to you in penitence for your forgiveness; in helpless weakness for your strength; in perplexity and doubt for your direction.

He that is down needs fear no fall,
He that is low, no pride;
He that is humble ever shall
Have God to be his guide.   *John Bunyan*

Father, I rest in your promises:
   that you will guide me daily into the way of peace;
   that your Holy Spirit will reveal to me the truth — truth about
      yourself, about the meaning of my life, and the purpose of
      your creation;
   that you will keep me in the path of righteousness;
   that you will give me the power to do the things you ask me to
      do, especially to show others your redeeming love in Jesus.

In the bewildering maze of events, emotions, duties and interests that make up my life, help me to know that there is a Way that leads to your immediate presence and that Way is the one man called Jesus of Nazareth; make me sure that there is meaning and purpose in my everyday life: in all that I shall do today; and that the purpose is benign, creative and good; so that at the end I may attain eternal peace and joy.

Lord, I put my hope in you;
  I have trusted in you since I was young.
I have relied on you all my life;
  you have protected me since the day I was born.
I will always praise you.   (*Psalm 71.5-6, GNB*)

O God, I give you thanks that
    in all the bewildering events of life I can be sure of your un-
    changing goodwill towards me;
    I can put myself in your hands this day to choose my path for
    me;
    I can trust to your gracious wisdom all I am and all I have, so
    that it is impossible to drift beyond your love and care.

Recall the times when you have relied upon the promises of God
and have found your confidence in him rewarded.

Bring before his throne of grace those things which make you feel
afraid, perplexed, depressed, guilty; and ask him for courage to
meet those things that daunt your spirit; direction in those affairs
in which the way seems dark; deep and lasting joy even in
circumstances which you have found depressing; absolution from
that which brings a sense of guilt.

Father, as your child, may I this day be free from too much
concern for wordly things. Help me to keep a right balance
between doing my duty faithfully in the day to day events of my
life, and being beguiled by the consumer society and over-fond of
riches. Make me always mindful that I can cast my care on you,
so that I may be ready to share the burdens of others.

Lord God, in whom, down the ages, so many have effectually
placed their trust: apostles, prophets, saints, and martyrs, along
with that great company whose names have no memorial;
encouraged by their example, I come to you with confidence to
ask that this day:
    though my hold on you may be insecure,
        yet you will firmly keep your hold on me;
    though I may not reach complete certainty,
        my faith in your good providence may be unswerving;
    though I do not look for safety in earthly things,
        my loyalty to you may remain unshaken.

Father, into your hands I commit my spirit.

Spend time in silent contemplation of the goodness of God in your life.

Praise, glory, wisdom, thanksgiving, honour, power, and might belong to our God for ever and ever!

> *When all thy mercies, O my God,*
> *My rising soul surveys,*
> *Transported with the view, I'm lost*
> *In wonder, love and praise.*   *Joseph Addison*

Give thanks to God
> for the victory over sin and death which he gives us through Jesus Christ;
> for the revelation of the grace of God which has come to us through Jesus: his free, undeserved and universal love;
> for the watchful, loving care of God for his children, and the immense value he sets upon each individual one of us.

Lord, I am grateful for all the goodness which in your mercy has brought me to this time and place;
> for the comfort of family and friends that you in your bounty have conferred upon me;
> for all that I have learnt from the minds of others through speech, the printed word, radio and television;
> for your gift of life itself; for reason, co-ordinating my senses and grasping ideas, and for setting me in a world that is full of your glory.

Accept, I pray, my thanksgiving for the hunger you have placed in my heart that can only be satisfied by communion with yourself;
> for the salvation won for me by Jesus, and the place you have given me in the fellowship of your Church.

Grant that I may learn
> how to use your gifts aright, especially those that link me with those I love, and meet, and work with;
> to show my thankfulness by living in accordance with your will;
> to be grateful for your comfort in trouble and companionship in joy.

For your encouragement and invitation to come boldly to your throne of grace for help in time of need, I thank you, Lord.

*Give thanks to God that all his promises are reaffirmed and ful-
filled in Jesus Christ, his Son, and that he has:*
    made us sure of life in union with Christ;
    set us apart to serve, worship, and love him;
    placed the mark of his ownership upon us;
    *and given us the Holy Spirit in our hearts as the guarantee of all
        that he has in store for us.*

                        (See 2 Corinthians 1.19-23, GNB)

Father, you know how much I need your help today; I need your
forgiveness and your healing; I need your guidance and direction;
your illumination for my mind, and inspiration for my spirit:
grant me your help.

Master, you know what I want and desire; do not give me
anything that is not in line with your will:
    you know my truest needs: fulfil them, I pray;
    you sent me here for a purpose: may I fulfil that purpose to the
        full extent of my powers.
I adore you for your mighty power, your wisdom, unfailing good-
    ness, pure unbounded love, and amazing humility.
I give thanks for the fellowship I find in your Church, and its
    sense of mission; help me to see that true service must be
    offered in your name.

Be with me in every difficulty I have to face; keep me obedient;
    teach me to forgive others even as I hope to be forgiven; give me
    the certainty of your guidance every step of my way, a sure trust
    in your abiding love, and a thankful heart that sees you as the
    fulfilment of God's promises and accepts your restraining,
    cleansing, uplifting, energising love with joy.

> *Jesus, if still the same thou art,*
>   *If all thy promises are sure,*
> *Set up thy kingdom in my heart,*
>   *And make me rich, for I am poor:*
> *To me be all thy treasures given,*
> *The kingdom of an inward heaven.*

                                  Charles Wesley

THE CHRISTIAN YEAR

Advent

Father, may this season of Advent renew our hope and the trust which we place in the future that you have prepared for us.
> May our hope be strong in the face of all that makes for despair, fear and unbelief:
>> the cruelties that people inflict on one another,
>> the questions that cannot be answered,
>> the uncertainty of our tomorrows.
> May our trust grow stronger, Father, as we celebrate the coming of Christ in glory,
>> when pain, suffering, parting and death will come to an end,
>> wars shall cease, hunger be no more,
>> and everyone live secure in your eternal love.

Forgive, Father, all within us that is unprepared for Christ's coming:
> our neglect of other people's need,
> our involvement in what is trivial and our indifference to what is of lasting importance in our lives,
> our idleness in prayer and our lack of attention to your word.

Make us ready for his coming that we may run to meet him with love, adoration and gratitude.

We pray for all who wait for Christ with longing, especially those who endure hardship and injustice.
We pray for —
> those who live under the shadow of tyranny who await the day when Christ will set them free;
> those whose bodies are weak with suffering who yearn for the Christ who will make them whole;
> those whose dreams have died who look for a Christ who will make possible what seems to be impossible;
> all who hunger and thirst for righteousness' sake.

Father, with the Church in every century we pray —
> Come, Lord, come.

Christmas

Thank you, Father, for this loved and familiar season:
>   for tuneful carols,
>   for reunions with families and friends,
>   for giving and receiving,
>   for a sense of celebration everywhere,
>   for all the ways of saying, 'Christ is born'.

We ask that the familiarity of Christmas may not smother the truth that we celebrate together.

May Christ be amongst us, as real, as close, as warm as at that first Christmas:
>   with Mary, may we open our hearts to the word of God, that Christ may be born in us;
>   with the shepherds, may we hear in the world of our daily work what heaven is saying to us;
>   may our experience of Christ be as real and enduring as theirs.

Save us from a faith so shallow that we put away our Christian commitment with the decorations or discard it like an unwanted present.

Father, hear our prayers for those for whom Christmas brings added responsibilities and tensions:
>   those who work throughout the holidays: hospital staff, energy workers, police, firemen, travel workers;
>   those who find Christmas increases the unhappiness they already have to carry: the lonely, divided families, the ill, those separated from the people they love, the depressed and anxious;
>   those who face the first Christmas following a bereavement.

Father, in Christ you embrace our happiness and our need: give to us a love that shall exclude none.

Epiphany

Father, we celebrate the coming of Jesus as the Light of the world:
let his light be in our minds that it may scatter the shadows of
our unreason, our confusion, our resistance to the truth;
let there be light in our behaviour, freeing us from all selfishness, unworthy deeds, ungenerous acts, and the thoughtless-
ness that brings pain to others;
let the light shine in our hearts and Christ's love reach every
part of our lives.

We would join in the homage of the Magi,
sharing with them in the light of Christ.
We present the homage of gold, Lord,
our obedience to our heavenly king,
our service in his kingdom.
We present the homage of frankincense,
our worship through Christ our priest,
who prays with us and for us.
We present the homage of myrrh, Lord,
the sign of sacrifice,
our longing to love as Christ loved.

Today we remember the baptism of our Lord:
Father, may we stand with him alongside all who seek the
coming of your kingdom.
Help us to commit ourselves in faith and obedience to whatever tasks you ask of us,
going wherever you send us,
answering whenever you call us.
Keep us loyal to the vows we have made;
may our faith lose none of its ardour with the passing years:
as we began, so may we continue, and end in you.

Ash Wednesday and Lent

Father, give to us the aid of your Holy Spirit
    that we may wisely use this season of Lent.
    It would be tempting, Lord, to make empty gestures, going
        without sugar, or cigarettes, or elevenses, dramatising what
        we do, giving it the appearance of sacrifice.
Father, if you would have us fast,
    then help us to be modest in our fasting,
    keeping what we do to ourselves,
    and not parading abstinence as a virtue for others to see and
        congratulate.
Help us to seek a deeper fellowship with Christ:
    may we read the scriptures with greater care,
    recognising those words that particularly speak to us,
    calling us to a greater obedience
    and more willing sacrifice;
    create within us a thirst for prayer,
    so that we may make more time to be with you,
    to listen for your voice in the silence,
    to renew our faith and love.
Help us to be more compassionate to others,
    to draw nearer to you by drawing nearer to them.
Father, may Lent teach us to be better Christians.

Lord, help us to put right in our lives those things we know to be
wrong:
    help us to be in control of our tongues so that we say nothing
        that will wound others needlessly, nor pass on half-truths or
        idle gossip, nor profess truth we do not believe;
    help us to be in control of our appetites, Lord, so that we may
        not eat more than is good for us, nor eat, careless of other
        people's hunger;
    help us to be in control of our desires, that wanting may not
        make us greedy or covetous.
Lord, may we not be swallowed up by our own ambitions.
May our needs be simple,
    our desires modest,
    our life-style Christ-like.

Lord Jesus, you were forty days in the wilderness,
    the place of tempting,
    the place of silence and prayer,
    the place of decision:
help us not to fear any wilderness through which we are called to
pass.
In the wilderness of temptation may we trust in the strength
    which you give us to resist the evils that seduce us.
In the wilderness of silence may we be still,
    waiting for your voice,
    free from anxiety and fretfulness.
In the wilderness of decision may we be given wisdom to choose
    what is good and right and in keeping with your will.

Lord, thank you for this time of spiritual renewal:
    we so often complain that we have no time,
    no time to pray,
    no time to listen;
    we rush about in our busyness,
    complaining that time is against us.
Lord, you have given us forty days of Lent:
help us not to waste them.

Holy Week

Palm Sunday

Welcome, Lord! With palms we strew your way
and with songs we greet you.
You come to us in peace, not as our enemy but as our friend, not
to make war but to reconcile, not to destroy but to heal.
You come to the city where there is tension and danger, where
ideas fly like arrows and men hunt for power.

Lord, you have chosen to come in peace,
armed with the strength of love:
let us, with you, work to bring
peace where there is war,
healing where there is division,
and compassion where there is hatred.

Come to our cities, Lord,
with their problems of over-crowding,
vandalism, violence, loneliness, poverty,
political neglect and stress:
come to rescue us from all that is destructive
and help us to work for the good of everyone.

Monday before Easter

Lord, you drove out of the temple those who commercialised their
religion and put business before prayer. We sometimes need your
love to drive out from the church those things that are unworthy
of your calling. Cleanse us from all status-seeking, from too much
concern for material welfare, from activity that is neglectful of
worship and prayer. May the church be a house of prayer for
everyone, open and welcoming to all.

Tuesday before Easter

Lord, may our homes be as open to you as the home at Bethany.
May every guest be received as Christ. May we live together in the
harmony of those who are privileged to serve you and to sit at your
feet listening to your word. May we be a refuge to one another in
times of distress and an encouragement in times of adversity.

Wednesday before Easter

Lord, in that last week you said so many brave things. You seemed unconcerned for your own safety. In dispute you held unswerving to the truth, you did not silence it in the face of those who threatened you.

Help us to be loyal to the truths in which we believe.

May no fear of scorn, indifference or hostility keep us from saying what sometimes has to be said.

May the uncertainty of what others might say or do not determine what we say or do.

You have called us to carry the cross, Lord — help us when it is heavy.

Maundy Thursday

We thank you, Lord, for giving to us today
    a way of remembering you,
    and a way of sharing in your love.
You invite us to gather around a table
    to break bread
    and to drink wine:
    and, in breaking, to recall that we are Christians because
        your body was broken for us upon the cross,
    and, in drinking, to recall that our sins are forgiven and our
        hurts are healed through the offering of your life.
May we come to communion, Lord,
    expectantly, gratefully and full of adoration.
Give us faith,
    that we may discern your presence
      in broken bread,
      in wine,
      and in the gathered body of your people.
Let each communion bring us nearer to you;
    grant that we who have known you
    in the simplicity of bread and wine,
    may discern you in every part of life.

Good Friday

Words are hard to find on this day, Lord:
>   what words can measure the height, depth, and breadth of
>   your love?
>   Before your agony, what can we say?
>   What prayer can we offer to you in this moment when God is
>   nearer and further away than anywhere else on earth?
Accept our prayers, Lord,
>   for all who suffer,
>   all who are in pain,
>   all who are unjustly condemned,
>   all who feel forsaken,
>   all who are dying.
By this cross, you are present in the deepest darkness.
May it be penetrated by the light of your presence.
Bring those for whom we pray through darkness to your ever-
    lasting day.

Holy Saturday

Lord, this is the day after and the day before.
Yesterday we died with you. Tomorrow we shall rise with you.
Now is the time in between.
Be with us, Lord, when we have lost what we had and have not yet
found peace, assurance and faith.
When yesterday's memories are more real than tomorrow's
resurrection, keep us strong in hope and trust.
Do not forsake us, Lord.

Easter

Father, it is the third day, the day for which all creation has waited:

> Christ is risen!
> Alleluia! He is risen indeed! Alleluia! Alleluia!

We pray that today's good news may reach the ears of men and women in every part of the world. May they see that evil has not conquered good, nor has hatred proved stronger than love, nor the light been overcome by the darkness. Father, we ask that this resurrection which is for all of us may be re-enacted over and over again in countless human hearts. May people see that it is precisely the things they fear most — pain, suffering at its most senseless, and death itself — that can become the womb out of which new life is given.

Bless your Church today, Father.
May your people grow in faith as they recount again the story of Christ's resurrection. Out of the pages of the scriptures, and in the ringing alleluias of the Easter hymns, may there grow a new confidence, a deeper awareness that we hold in our hands the keys of the kingdom of heaven.

Forgive us, Father, all that denies resurrection: our moods of despair, our unwillingness to persevere, our desire to have life without death, love without sacrifice. Forgive us our timidity whenever we lock up our faith behind the closed doors of fear or tradition, refusing to face the world and its challenge. May Christ stand among us and, in forgiving us, breathe his peace into our hearts.
Lift us up on the eagle's wings of this day, O Lord, that we may live with Christ forever.

Ascension

Father, today you received our Lord Jesus Christ in the embrace
    of paradise,
  exalted him to your right hand in glory everlasting,
  took him from our sight, though no longer from our side.

We remember with thanksgiving the commission he gave to us
and the promise he made to us.
He called us to witness to the world, Father. We pray for the
courage to obey that commission. May we never withhold your
word from our fellow-men, either through neglect of our duty or
lack of compassion. Though we be faced with agnosticism and
unbelief, though our witness seem to beat against the indifference
of others, yet still may we trust the power of your spirit to lead
people into the fullness of Christ and his kingdom.

We remember with thanksgiving the promise of his presence with
us until the end of the world.
He is here with us now, Father. In all the varied circumstances in
which our lives are set, may we know Christ beneath us, above us,
behind us, before us and at our side. May loneliness be banished,
may our fears be quelled, because he is here. Let Christ's
presence give to our words and actions a boldness and a
compassion they would not otherwise possess.

You received Jesus into your glory, Father.
Teach us that this is our destiny, too. May we not love earth so
much that we lose sight of heaven, may our affections not be so
firmly fixed on the world that is, that we do not grow towards the
world that is to come.

We thank you that Jesus shall come again and, on that day,
creation will sing for joy.

Pentecost

Father, we bless you for pouring out your Holy Spirit upon the
 Church:
 for the free wind that sweeps through the world,
 for the tongues of fire, signs of ardour, warmth and love,
 for words to praise and proclaim you,
 for hearts opened to receive you.

Bless your Church in every part of the world, Father:
 bless those who are young in faith that they may be open to all
  the possibilities of life in Christ and may grow in knowledge
  and maturity;
 bless those who witness in areas of great human need, where
  there is hunger or poverty, political unrest and civil strife,
  violence and the threat of war;
 bless our brothers and sisters in places where the Church is
  persecuted and they are made to suffer for the faith they
  profess;
 bless those who witness in areas where the Church is growing
  and people daily are being added to the Church.
Father, may your Spirit be active among them all
 to nurture the young,
 to strengthen the needy,
 to uphold the oppressed
 and to inspire all who testify.

Breathe the Spirit into our hearts, Father.
Set us free from habits or traditions that no longer allow the Spirit
to move freely among us. Touch our tongues with holy fire that we
may more effectively proclaim the gospel. Fill all our activities
with the love of Christ that what we do may serve the increase of
your kingdom.
Father, give us the Spirit and help us to receive him.

Trinity

Lord, we acknowledge that you are our God,
    One everlasting Lord,
    Father, Son and Holy Spirit.

O God, Father and Creator, we worship you.
    You brought the earth to birth,
    called the morning sun out of the night,
    clothed the darkness with moon-light,
    spread the earth with verdure,
    plunged the fish into the seas, released the birds into the skies,
        peopled the earth with creatures great and small,
    made man in your own image.

O God, the Son, Lord Jesus Christ,
    you came to us in our flesh and blood,
    in your words we have heard God's word,
    in your deeds the kingdom has come among us,
    in your death our death has been died,
    in your resurrection eternal life given to all of us:
    you dwell in the glory of the Godhead,
    Light of light, God of God,
    Bread of heaven, Fountain of life.

O God, the Holy Spirit,
    you have come among us as wind and fire,
    you have liberated our tongues to praise you,
    you have shared your gifts among us that together we might be
        the people of God,
    it is your radiance that falls upon the scriptures,
    it is your voice that prays within us,
    it is you who sets us free.

Lord God, Father, Son and Holy Spirit, we worship and adore
you.

SPECIAL OCCASIONS

Special days

The Week of Prayer for Christian Unity

Father, you have shown us that we worship one Lord, share in one faith and have received one baptism. We cannot afford the luxuries either of walking away from one another in self-righteousness or of fighting one another. We pray that our zeal for unity in Christ may not be a once-yearly burst of energy that burns itself out in a week. May we constantly seek ways of growing, witnessing, praying and serving together. May love for our fellow-Christians grow the more we come to know them. Teach us what it means to be the body of Christ.

Church Anniversary

Father, out of two thousand years of Christian history we celebrate this small part to which our own church belongs.

> Thank you for those through whose vision and industry our church was founded in this place.

> Thank you for the generations that have gone before us, ensuring that there has been no moment when Christ has been without his witnesses.

We ask, Father, that we may be no less faithful than were they. As we have given thanks for past witness so may those who follow have cause for gratitude to us.

Missionary Sunday

Lord, the world has changed so much since the days of the missionary pioneers. We have become a global village. Familiarity has robbed the missionary cause of some of its romance, excitement and challenge.

> Teach us that there is much that has not changed.

> There is hunger and there is injustice.

> The sick cry for healing and everywhere man pursues his age-old search for God.

Lord, you alone are the way, the truth and the life. Be with those who share your love with people of other nations. Grant that, through the diversity of their work, they may be the embodiment of the love they proclaim.

Harvest

Lord, there is joy in this season. The earth again has performed her miracle and out of the seed buried in darkness has brought to birth our daily bread.

Thank you, Lord, for rain and sun that have summoned the seed out of the earth.

Thank you for those who have harvested the crops and those who have brought them to us.

Thank you, Lord, for our food and drink.

Remembrance Sunday

Father, we remember today that freedom is bought at a terrible price: the price of men's blood.

We remember today that war, though it demands courage and sacrifice, is cruel, dirty, destructive and hateful.

We remember today that ordinary men and women were prepared to pay the price of their own lives and to endure the agony of battle.

Father, may we guard our peace with as much devotion as those who fought for it.

Bible Sunday

Father, may our love for the scriptures grow with our knowledge of them. We pray for preachers and teachers, that they may open to us the exciting and liberating truth contained in the Bible. We pray for biblical scholars, that we may welcome rather than fear their work as it helps us to understand the scriptures at greater depth. We pray for translators, that they may be accurate in their work and so share the gospel with a growing number of people.

We pray for ourselves, Father, that what we hear may influence what we are.

Special times

The birth of a child

Lord, this baby was conceived in our love, carried with love and is now welcomed with love. Thank you for the safe arrival of our baby.

Be with us, Lord, because we are suddenly aware of the enormous responsibility that is ours. Without our care, our support, our guidance, our child would not survive. Help us to accept our responsibility courageously and joyously. Guide us in the decisions that will be ours in the days to come. May our child grow in an atmosphere of security and loving acceptance. We will never be perfect parents — help us to be the best we can be.

Starting a new job

Lord, this is an exciting and anxious day.
So many questions —
   will I cope with the work?
   how will I get on with the others?
   have I made the right decision — have they?
Lord, help me to use the skills you have given to me.
May I enjoy this work, even when it is difficult or boring.
I am being paid to do this, Lord — help me to earn it.

An engagement

Father, we believe you have given us to each other. Out of all the people in the world, our paths have crossed, we have found each other and we love each other.

Help us to remember this day — the dreams, the happiness, the trust and the hope that now we share. May our dreams be turned into reality may our happiness be strong even in adversity, may our trust be honoured, and our hope fulfilled. We place a hand in each other's and both our hands in yours. We have each other and we have you, our love and your love. Father, we are so happy.

A wedding

Father, in the days of preparation there were times when we were almost in danger of forgetting what this day is all about. But now the danger is passed, the preparations are complete, our wedding day has come. Help us to enjoy today, Father, and to remember it as long as we shall live. Thank you for the families and friends who will share our happiness today. In the wedding service may we realise what we are promising each other and open our hearts to your grace and strength. May this day be but the beginning of a great happiness.

A wedding anniversary

Lord, today we thank you for each other. The years go so quickly and yet we know now that we are a part of each other.

We thank you for all the laughter we have shared, our private jokes, our funny habits.

We thank you for the times when we have been a strength to each other, for what we might have lacked apart we found together.

We thank you for the day by day adventure of being man and wife — for the companionship, help and comfort that we have given to each other.

There's more yet. Help us to grow closer to each other and to you in everything that is yet to be.

Retirement

Lord, today I close the longest chapter of my life and begin a new one. Thank you for the years of work and all that they meant to me — the people with whom I shared them, the daily routine and whatever I was able to achieve.

Be with me in the days to come. May I find new fulfilment in the freedom and leisure that will now be mine. There are so many things I said I would do, if only I had the time. Time I now have — help me to use it to the full.

Bereavement

Lord, as the numbness passes the pain gets sharper. I expect to hear a familiar voice. I walk into a room, see an empty chair and can hardly hold back the tears. I turn to share something, an item of news, an anxiety, something I saw when I was out, and there is no one to share it with. I don't want to be eaten up with self-pity but, Lord, I need your pity. I'm not asking to be brave, just to survive this awful emptiness — this grief. They tell me that one day the pain will get easier, one day I will finally be able to let go. That day hasn't come yet, Lord. Until then, let me know that you are near me.

Special situations

Facing an examination

Lord, give me the physical and mental stamina to prepare for this exam. I don't normally have to work to the limits of my concentration, but in the coming days I may need to. Give me the discipline to complete the preparation I have set for myself. When the day of the exam comes may my excitement stimulate my mind and not confuse it. Help me to give of my best and not to be too overawed by the occasion. If I succeed keep me modest. If I fail may I not be defeated.

Moving house

Father, this has been my home and now I am leaving it. Thank you for the memories it holds and for the warmth and shelter it has provided. Now my possessions are packed away in boxes and I know what it feels like to be a pilgrim, travelling light and not quite knowing where he is going to lay his head. May this move teach me that all life is a journey and nowhere is permanent. Be with me in my new home. May I quickly come to feel a sense of belonging. Help me to adapt quickly to new neighbours, new surroundings, a new way of living.

Being ill

Lord, suddenly my body feels different, as if it doesn't belong to me any more. I'm used to being in control, but now the illness has taken over. Help me to accept this time of illness and to learn something from it. Help me to learn from my dependence upon others. Help me to accept what they do for me with gratitude but not to make my weakness an excuse for demanding so much that I drain their resources. Help me to accept the fact that I am not as brave as I thought I was. Above all, surround me with your peace and assurance that I may grow closer to you than I have ever been before.

In hospital

Lord, I thank you for the care and skill by which I am surrounded. May my body respond to what is being done for my healing. Give me peace when I am nervous. May relief and comfort be to hand when I am in pain. May each day bring a stronger sense of well-being as I recover. Bless the staff and help me to co-operate with them in all that they do for my good. Be with my fellow-patients, help me to share their condition, to help those who are weaker, and gratefully accept the support of those who are stronger than I am. May this experience bring me nearer to you.

A family celebration

Father, you who are head of all our families, we thank you that you share our happiness with us. We thank you that Jesus was the guest at many parties and brought a sense of celebration with him. May he be with us, the most honoured guest in our party. Because he is here may we accept one another, responding to one another's presence, grateful for one another's joy. Make this a memorable party, Lord, one that we shall remember on ordinary, uneventful days. So may every day have cause for thanksgiving, and every meal become something of a celebration.

A holiday thanksgiving

Lord, it's been bliss:
   a break from routine,
   no dead-lines to meet,
   different surroundings, different people,
   a few days without any pressures.
The world looks different from here:
   may it look different when I go back,
   less fraught, more joyous,
   may I see the old, familiar faces in a new light.
May home welcome me like an old friend.

General thanksgiving

Father, may I never grow ungrateful for the life that you have given me, nor despairing of its possibilities. May I never grow cynical about the world in which you have set me. May each day be welcomed as a new opportunity and each person as the neighbour whom Christ has given me. Thank you for people, for city streets and lonely mountains, for streams on a hillside and rain on window panes, for the seasons, for sun and cloud, for words, conversations, books, jokes, prayer, for music that lifts me close to heaven and ordinary days that so often take me by surprise.

A birthday

Thank you for today, Lord, the anniversary of the day that I was born:
> thank you for my mother and father who gave me life and cared for me in my green years;
> thank you for the people who want to share the happiness of to-day with me, greeting me, celebrating my birth day with me;
> thank you for the changing years and all that they have taught me;
> thank you for all the people I have loved;
> thank you for all the people who have loved me;
> thank you for Jesus Christ, in whom I was given a second birth.

A parting

Father, it is always hard to say good-bye. We seem to spend our lives saying good-bye. Every stage of life is a farewell, a parting. We leave first one school and then another, we leave our home for the first time, we leave one group of friends and pass on to another, we leave our youth and enter our manhood or womanhood. And now we are saying good-bye again. Bless these friends we leave behind us; thank you for all that they mean to us. May there be times when the distance between us seems as nothing — when we write a letter, when we pray, when we are gathered for communion, and time and distance vanish in Christ.

A journey

Lord, deliver us —

> from hazards of the road — tyre blow-outs, over-heated engine, slippery roads, a car crash;
>
> from hazards of the air — faulty equipment, turbulent weather, hi-jackers;
>
> from hazards of the sea — tempest and storm;
>
> from hazards of the rail — late arrival, derailment, fog.

Lord, it might be safer to stay at home: but we have to take the risk if we are to go anywhere. Travelling, or faith itself, is always a dangerous business.

Deliver us from evil

Father, I am going through a bad time. The world seems hostile, nothing seems to be going right for me, I am beginning to lose my confidence. Help me now. May I learn through this experience that your love is stronger than the dangers that threaten me. May my weakness be the very means of discovering your strength. Christ died and rose again for all of us. I am going through a sort of dying. Help me to believe I shall rise again.

Various moods and needs

A time of happiness
Lord, we thank you for everything that brings us happiness in life. We pray that we may not fear happiness, or be anxious that what we have today we may lose tomorrow. Teach us to accept today's joys and leave tomorrow until it comes. May our happiness not make us selfish or isolate us from other people. Save us from the temptation of protecting our own happiness by refusing to be involved in the sorrows of other people. May happiness make us more open and vulnerable to others, not less. Glad in what we have received, may we be joyous in sharing it.

Reading a book
Lord, every day there is a small addition to the mountain of words that have been written. So many words, tumbling about us. It would be easy to say that too many is too much and refuse to listen to another word or read another book. Lord, may I not renounce this wealth by which I am surrounded, but use it with discretion. Help me to choose wisely what I read so that books may enlarge my outlook and not narrow it. May I not read only to confirm what I already believe but to challenge and extend my knowledge and my belief.

Listening to music
Lord, we thank you for those who write music and those who make music. For the vision of the composer, the glory of the sounds that he creates, the tunes he weaves out of his own soul, bringing into existence something that wasn't there before, we praise you. For the skill of musicians, the sheer marvel of what they do, we praise you. For music itself, that strange beauty, unseen, intangible, strong enough to lift us dumb-struck up to heaven, ordinary enough to sing in the bath, beautiful enough to make us glad to be alive, we praise you.

On reading the Bible

Father, we thank you for the holy scriptures and pray that you will guide us as we read them. May those parts that we know well come to mean more to us each time we read them. Give us the curiosity and courage to explore those parts that are as yet unknown territory. Help us to see our own humanity in the men and women who walk through the pages of scripture. As we listen to the words of prophets, priests and kings, may they ring with truth for our century as much as for the time in which they were written. Above all, we pray that we may hear you speaking to us, and in the story of Jesus see your presence among us.

A time of depression

Lord, there are shadows at the edge of my heart,
　　the darkness creeps nearer,
　　enemies lurk there, too vague to be resisted,
　　I can't think straight, logic has deserted me,
　　I fear my dreams, and dread waking early:
　　　　help me, Lord.
May I feel your strength beneath me when I fear that I am sinking.
May your light scatter the darkness where fear hides. Bring me out to daylight and resurrection.

A request for guidance

Lord, I need to make a decision and to know what you want me to do. There could be a blinding light from heaven, a sudden flash of inspiration, making clear beyond all doubt what I should choose. On the other hand, you are probably asking me to work this one out for myself. Help me to use what intelligence you have given me, to see all sides of the question. May what I know of the scriptures influence my decisions. May I listen to what is wise in the advice of my friends and be able to distinguish it from what is unwise. Give me your Holy Spirit, that he may work through my thinking and listening.

Getting on with other people

Father, you have made us all so different:
  in one way, this makes for friction, for we see things differently,
    our reactions, our beliefs, our background are all different;
  in another way, this makes for enrichment, for a world of so
    many different people means that there are countless
    different possibilities.
So we can fight, or we can co-operate.
Jesus said that fighting is out.
So help us to work together, Father.

Coping with disappointment

Lord, there are times when we set out with high hopes. There are
dreams that are going to come true, battles that are going to be
won, mountains conquered, situations changed, ambitions fulfilled. Then it goes wrong and we sit with the wreckage all around
us. Pick us up, Lord, and help us to start again. Perhaps it didn't
work out the way we had hoped. Perhaps you have some better
way.

Coping with anxiety

Father, be with us when we feel the weight of our responsibility.
We have decisions to make that are not always clear-cut and their
outcome may affect the happiness of other people. We fear what
tomorrow may hold and cannot be accurate in our predictions of
what will happen. The health, happiness and welfare of those we
love most sometimes makes us anxious. Father, into your hands
we commend all our responsibilities. Help us to know that we are
all carried in the hands of your love. May we be open to the
strength of your Spirit and better able to bear our responsibilities.

For a sense of humour

Lord, there will be laughter in paradise,
   and the laughter has begun on earth:
   so save us from being humourless
   lest we be unprepared for heaven.
May laughter put flight to the devil,
   may humour lighten the darkness,
   may our jokes be a way of learning your truth.
We do not pray for the grin of the Cheshire cat,
   but for a light heart, a ready wit,
   a blessed sense of humour.

Facing death

Father, there will come a day when I must die. I don't know how I shall feel when that day comes, as life drains from my body and I feel the only world I know drifting away from me. I can only begin to imagine what it feels like to die.

Father, when that day comes I ask that I may know you near me. As my strength leaves me may your love penetrate me. As this world passes from my sight may I see ever more clearly the world that awaits me at my death.

Father, may my death be resurrection in Christ.

Celebrating the faith

Going to church

Father, you gave us this first day of the week as a time to praise, to pray, to listen and to celebrate. Be with us as we go to your house; finding you there may we find you everywhere. We ask that our worship may be offered with love. May the offering of our heart have the assent of our mind and the submission of our will. May we allow our celebration to affect what we feel, what we think and what we do. May we hear the scriptures with eagerness, may our prayers be offered in the faith that you hear us and respond, may our singing be a joyous affirmation of our faith. Bless all strangers who come to your house, and may the warmth of your people ensure that they are not strangers when they leave.

A prayer before Communion

Lord, with love and expectancy we approach this sacred mystery. You call us to eat and drink together, celebrating the breaking of your body and the offering of your blood.
As it happened at Emmaus, so we ask that you be shown to us today in the breaking of bread. May your living presence surround us and be within us as we receive the sacrament. As we see our daily bread broken to fulfil your holy purposes so may we have the faith to see all ordinary things hallowed and made the means of your grace. May the glory of your risen presence all about us fill our hearts with love, our worship with joy, and our tomorrows with hope.

Prayer after Communion

Lord, you have given to us the bread of heaven. You gave it, not because we had earned or deserved it, but because your name is love and your delight is to give. As we have received, so may we share. As the bread was broken and given to your people, so may our gifts, our possessions, our concern, be shared with those whom you have called us to serve. As the wine was offered in celebration of your death and resurrection, so may our lives be a willing sacrifice and may we find our greatest happiness in offering up ourselves to your service. May every part of life be a celebration of your rising, and every day be lived in gratitude for your love.

Grace before meals

Lord, bless the labours that produced this food,
>   bless the skill that prepared it,
>   bless the bodies that receive it,
>   bless the people who share it,
>   bless the hungry and grant that one day
>>   all men everywhere may sit at the table of plenty.

Grace after meals

Lord, accept our thanks for this food that we have shared:
>   may we wisely use the strength it has given us,
>   may we increase in faith, knowing our prayers have been answered,
>   our daily bread given to us.

May we generously break the bread of our plenty and share it with our needy brothers and sisters.